knacker's yard

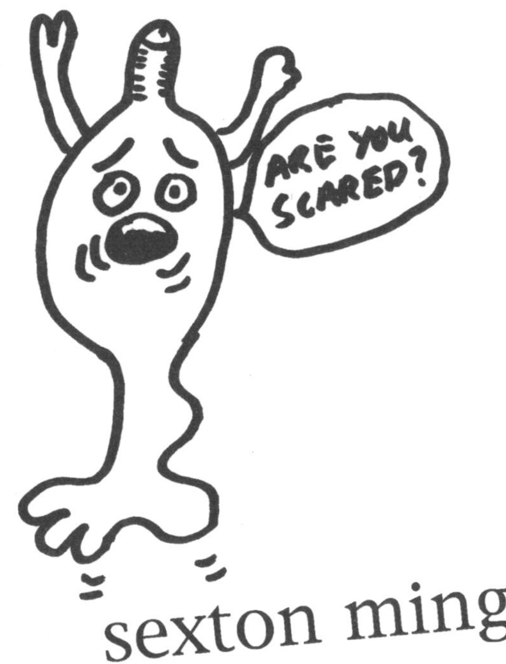

sexton ming

first edition

published by the aquarium, London 2006

printed by Mackays of Chatham
bound in 350gsm brown line chip card

first 100 copies complete with colouring-in crayons and
signed by the artist

www.theaquariumonline.co.uk

ISBN 1 871894 03 4

introduction

This is Sexton Ming's first ever mass market paperback and the first book ever to be devoted solely to his strange and wonderful drawings.

Ming is a writer/musician/painter extraordinaire and his meandering mind can take you on an otherworldly journey steeped in so much black humour, tangential weirdness and biting observation of the human race it makes this world a much better place. He is little known in mainstream culture but is in fact world famous. He was a founding member of the Medway Poets, has appeared on over 20 albums, painted some of the strangest paintings in the world, supported Sonic Youth live, was called a failed intellectual by Ralph Steadman and once saved Billy Childish's life.

We could write a lengthy discourse on how these simple little drawings are important to our increasingly dull and homogenised culture, and how they could in fact save the human race, but we'll save that for next time.

Welcome to the world of Sexton Ming

MONSTERS OF DEATH

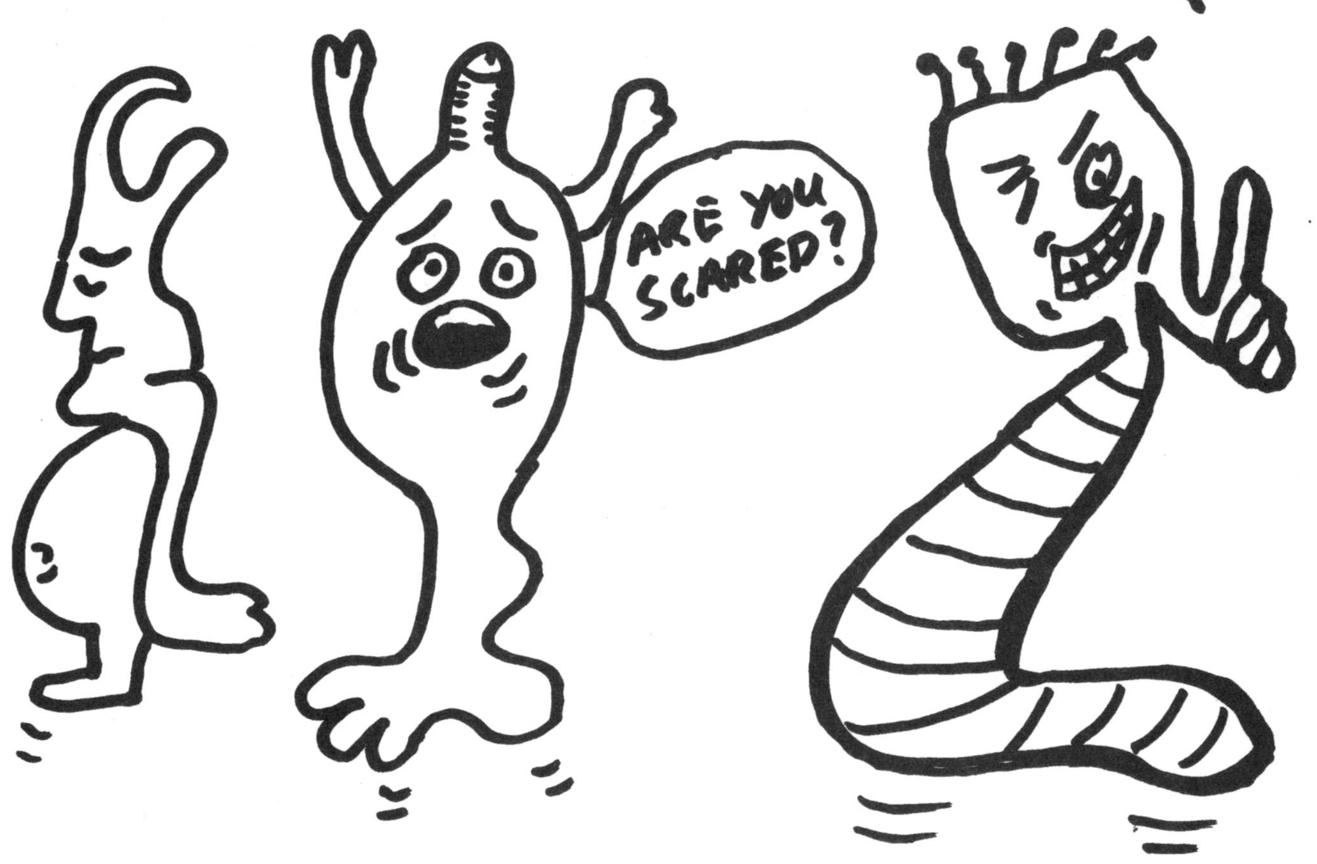

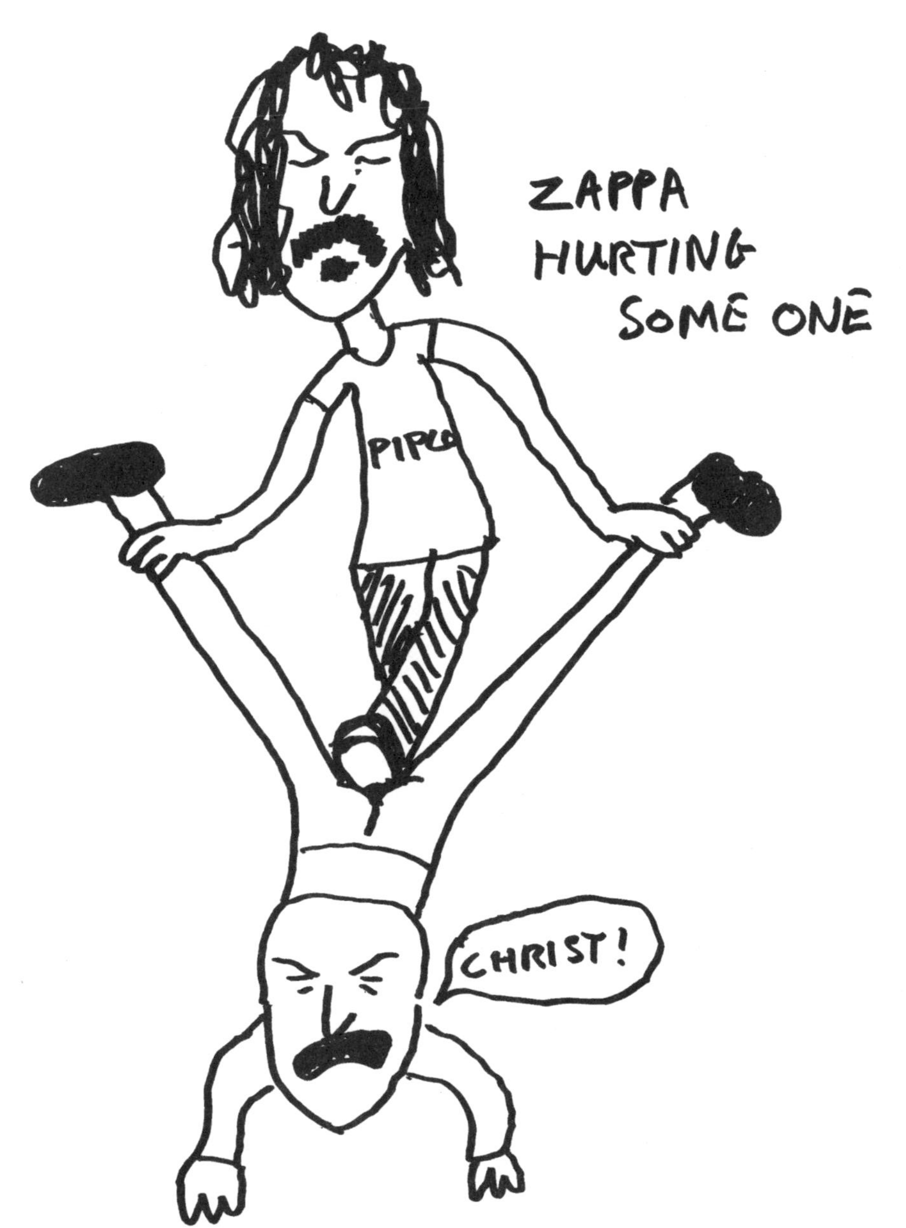
ZAPPA
HURTING
SOME ONE
PIPLO
CHRIST!

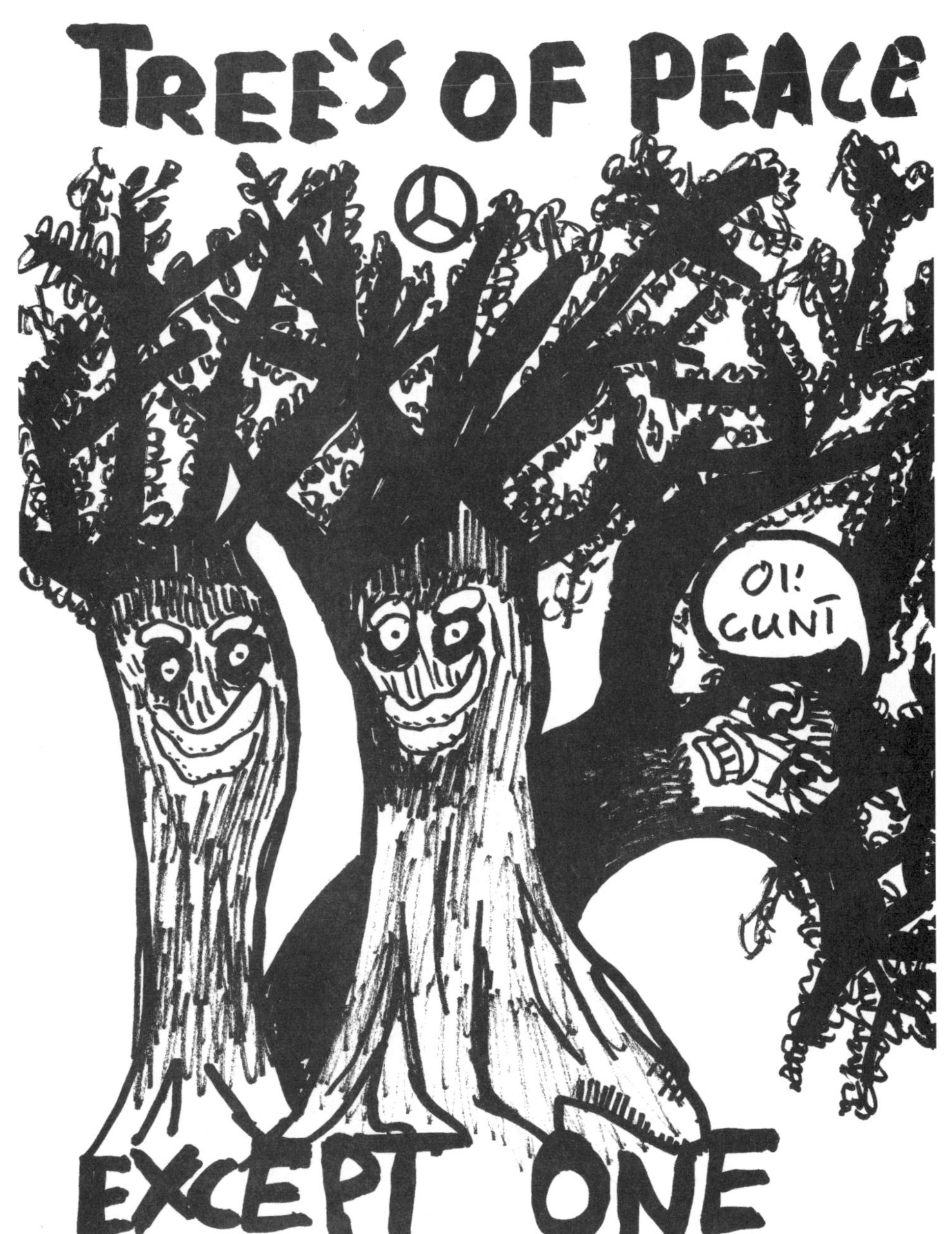
TREE`S OF PEACE
OI! CUNT
EXCEPT ONE

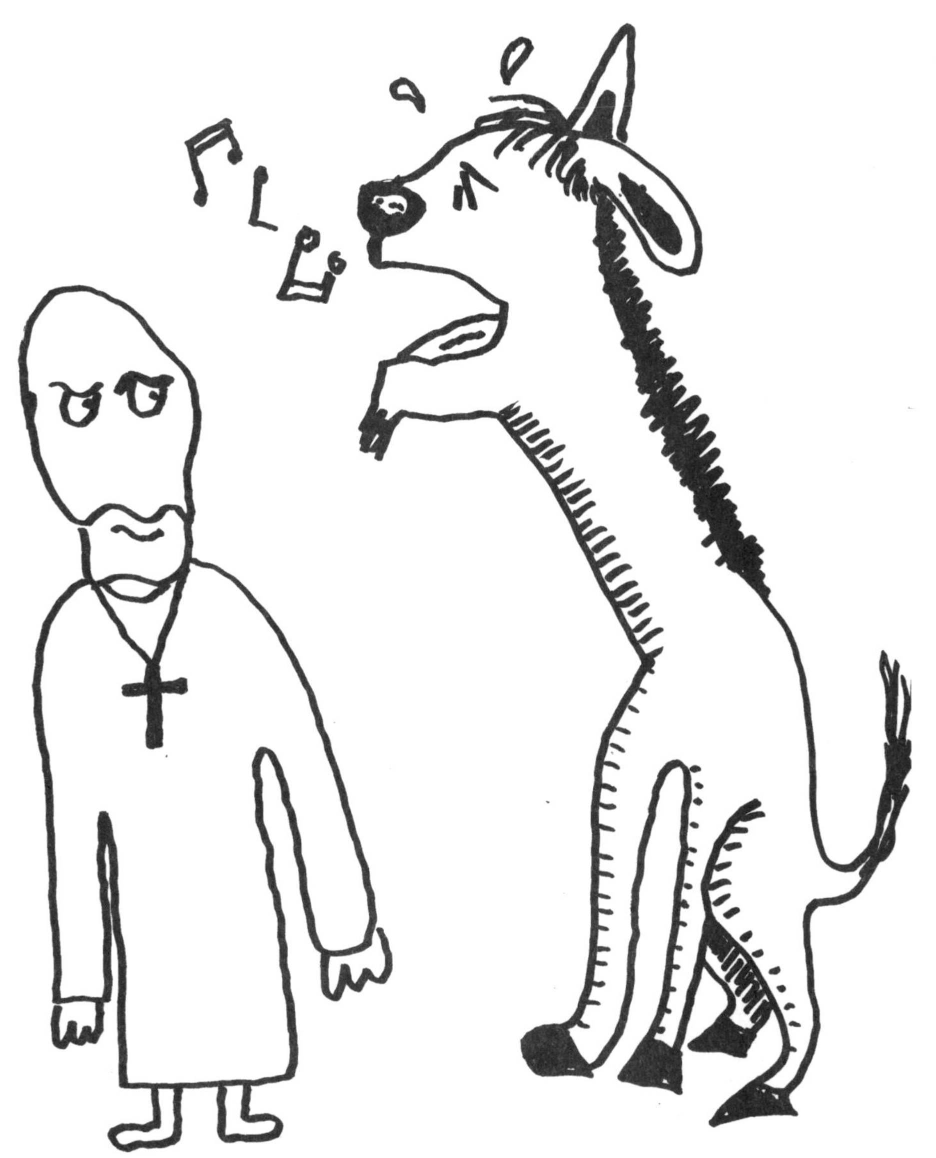

THE DONKEY SANG HIS HEART OUT

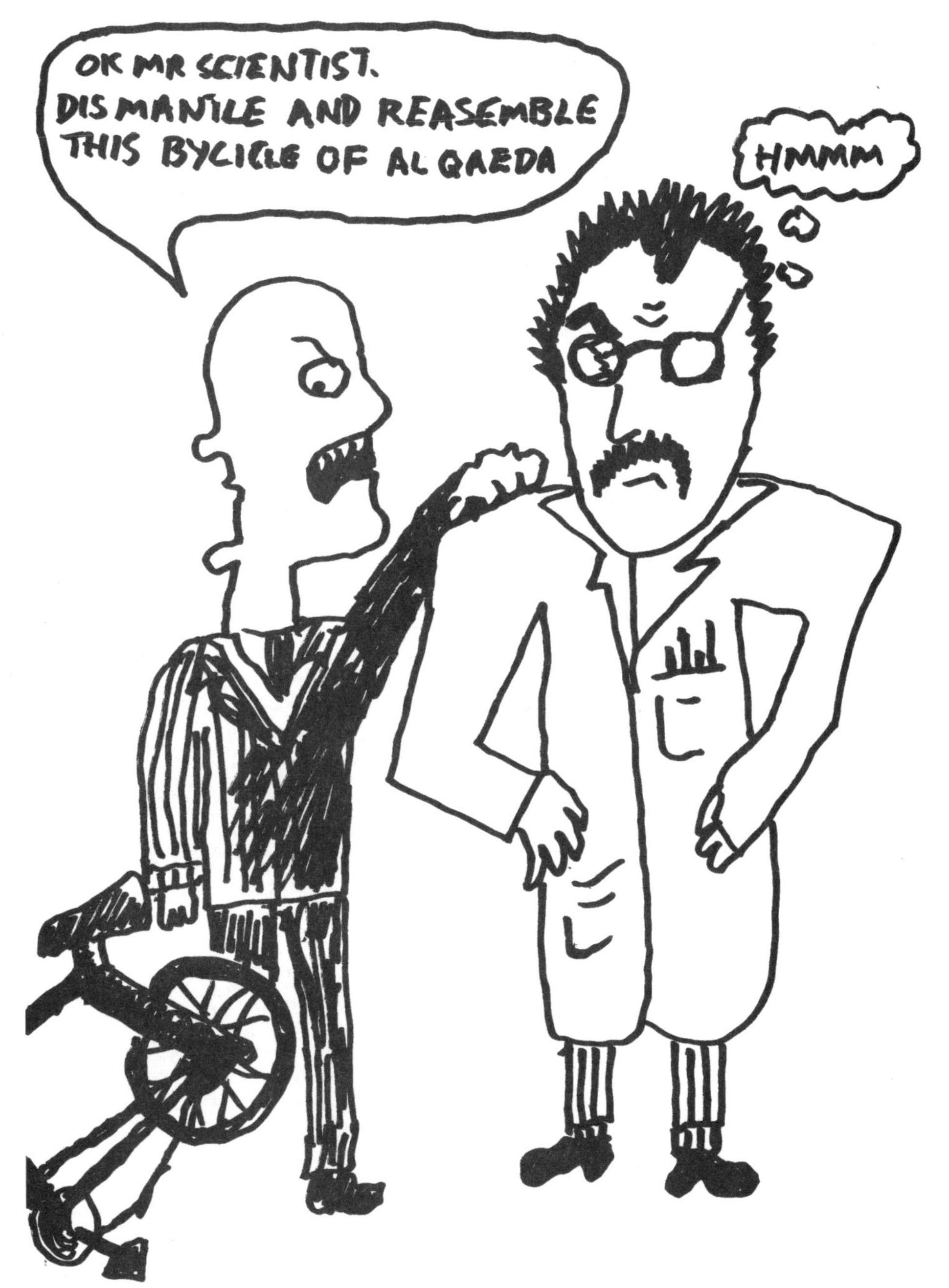
OK MR SCIENTIST.
DIS MANTLE AND REASEMBLE
THIS BYCICLE OF AL QAEDA
HMMM

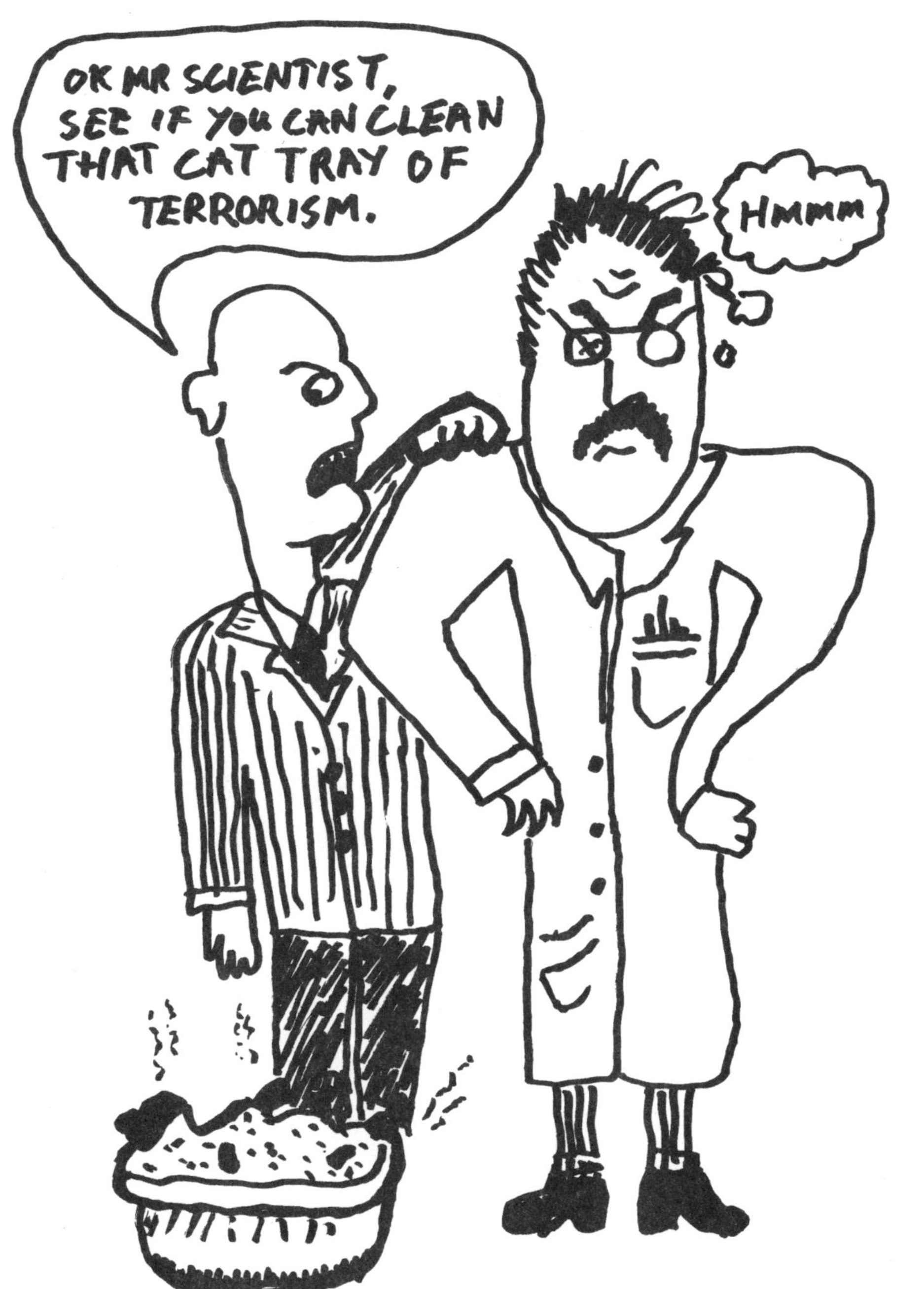
OK MR SCIENTIST, SEE IF YOU CAN CLEAN THAT CAT TRAY OF TERRORISM.
HMMM

SMELLY MAN HAS A THOUGHT

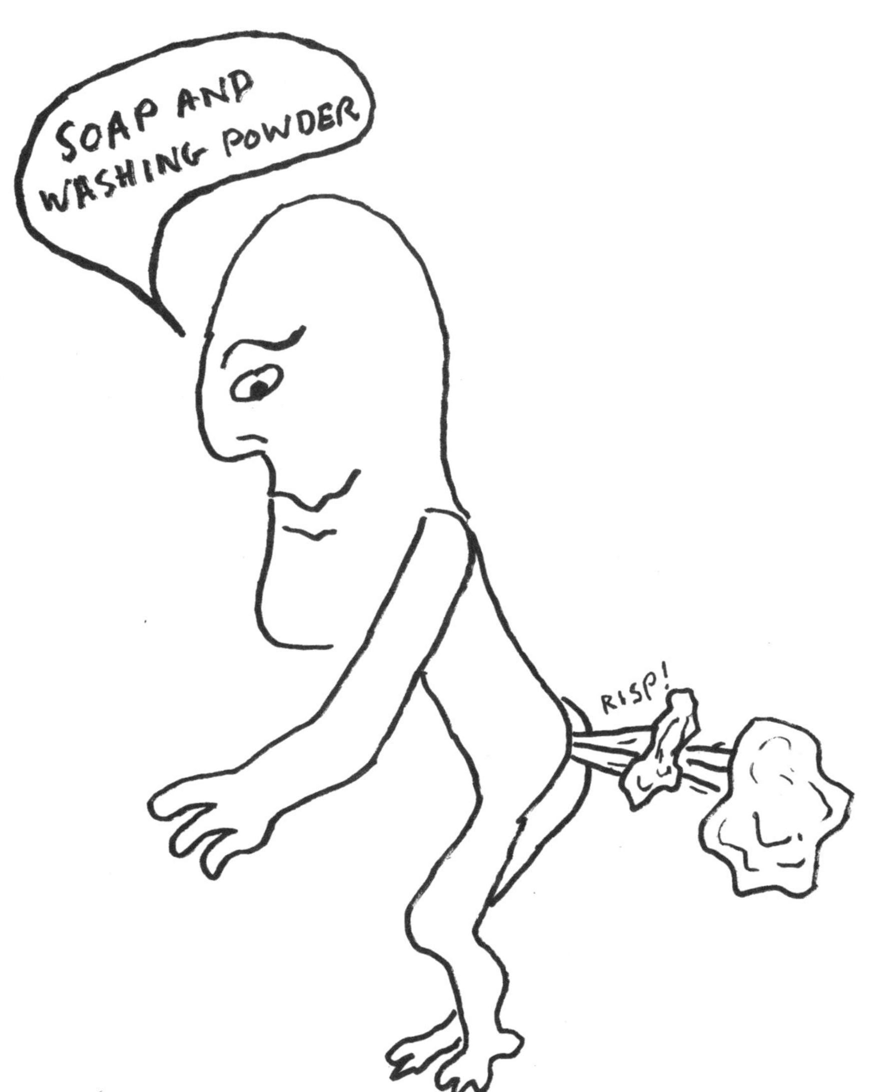

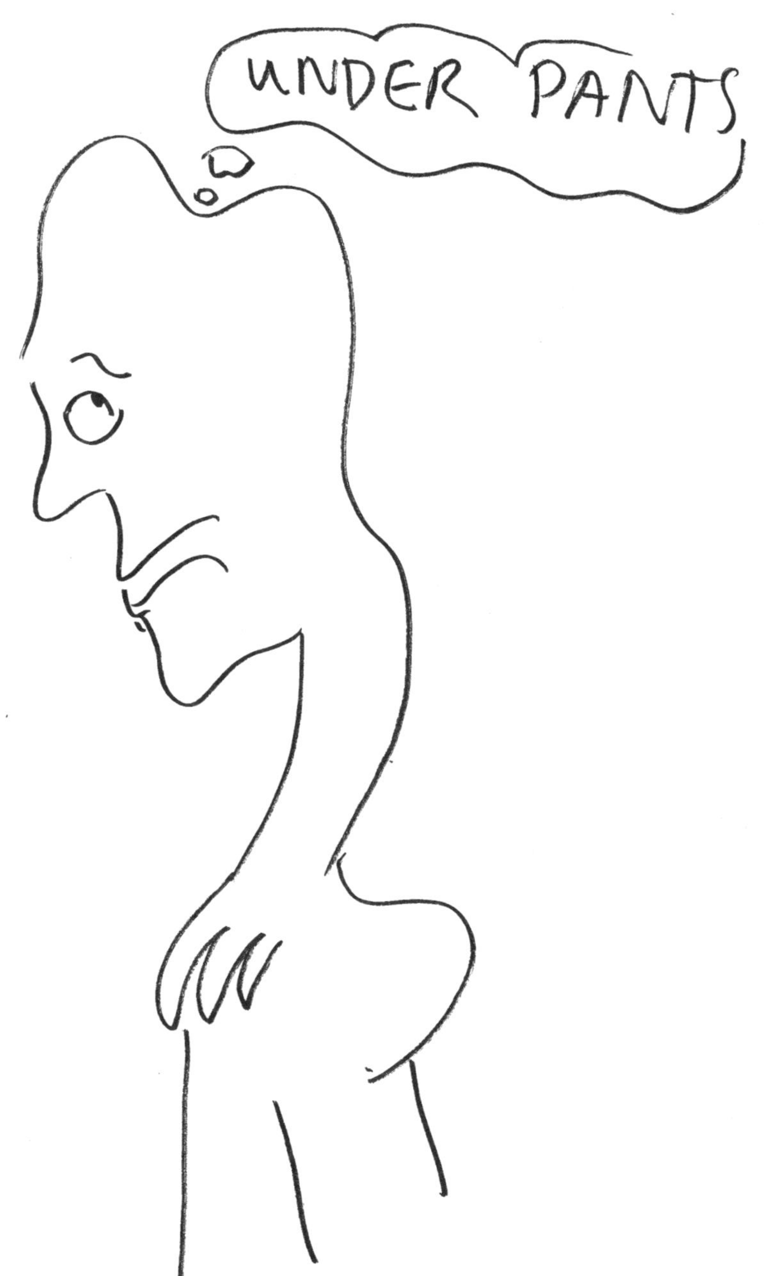
UNDER PANTS

WISE MUTT SAYS...

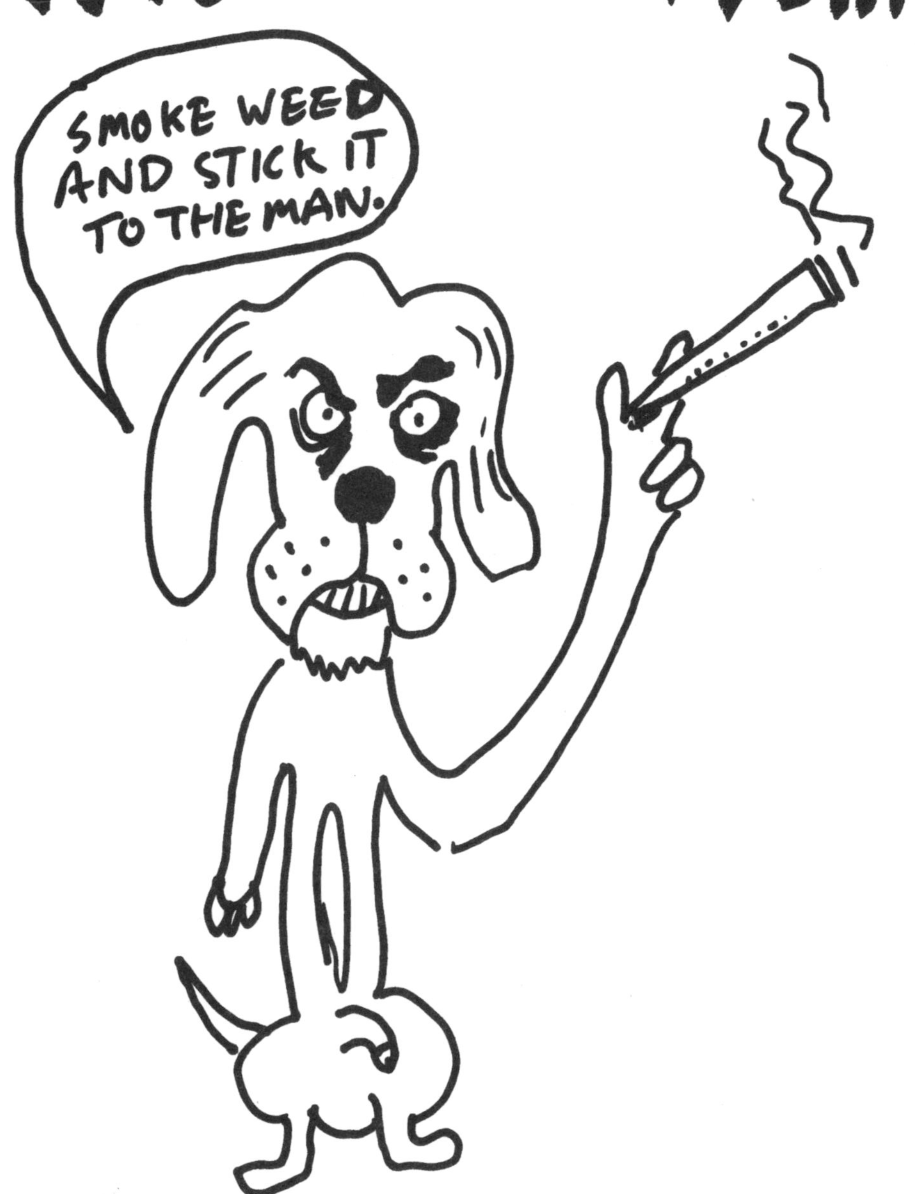

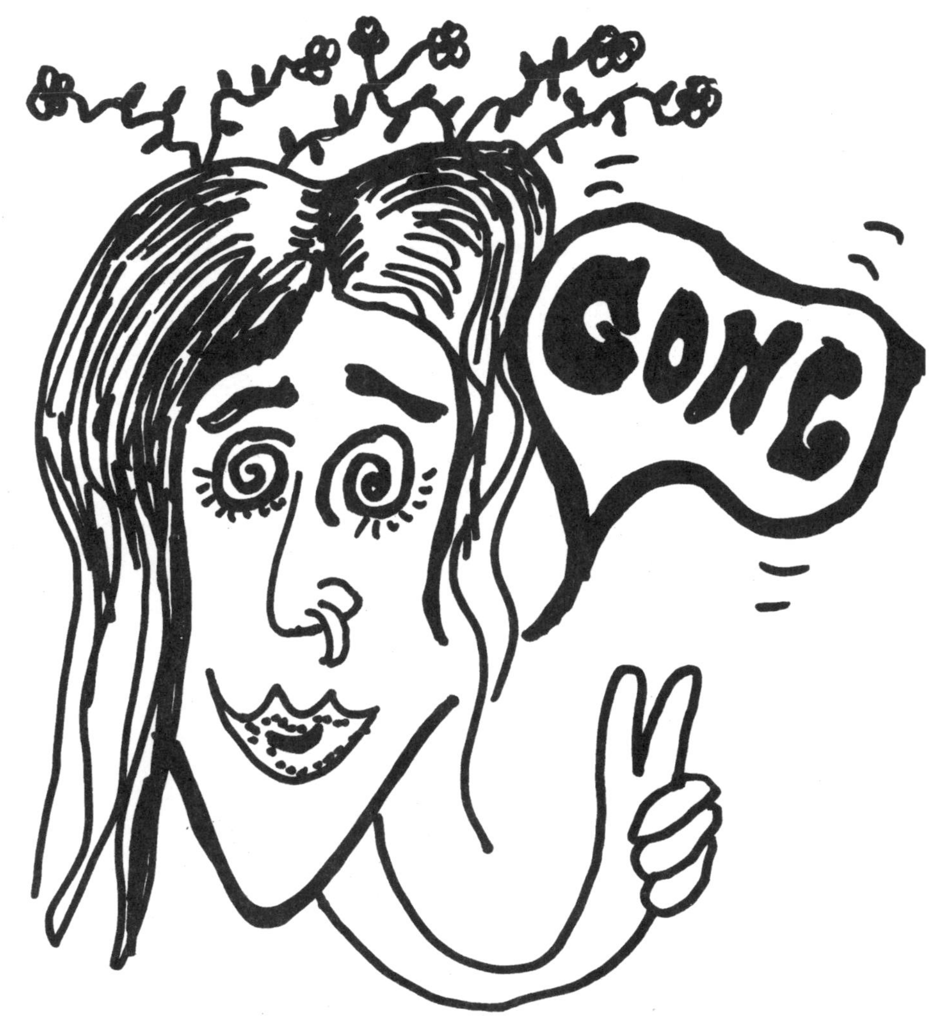

STONED UP WOMAN

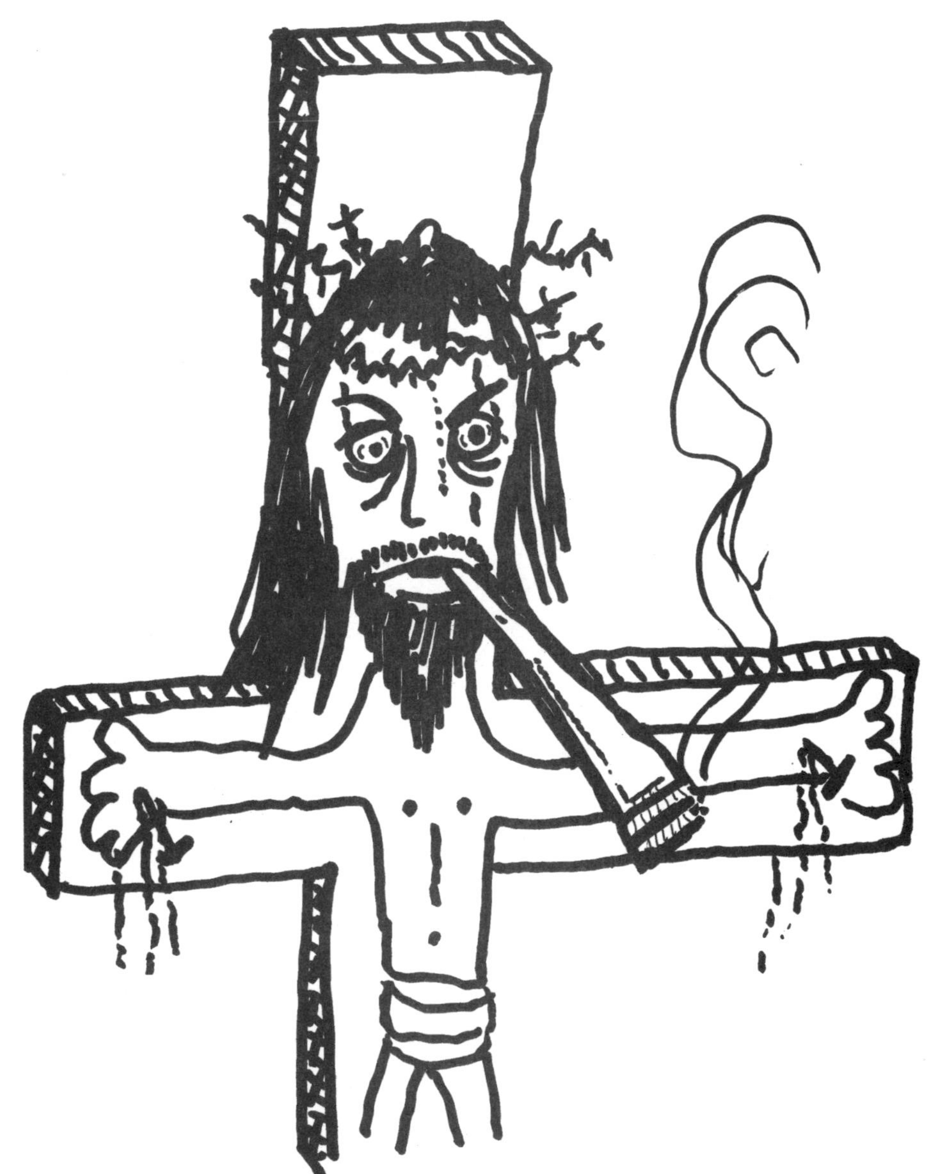

SKIN UP FOR JESUS

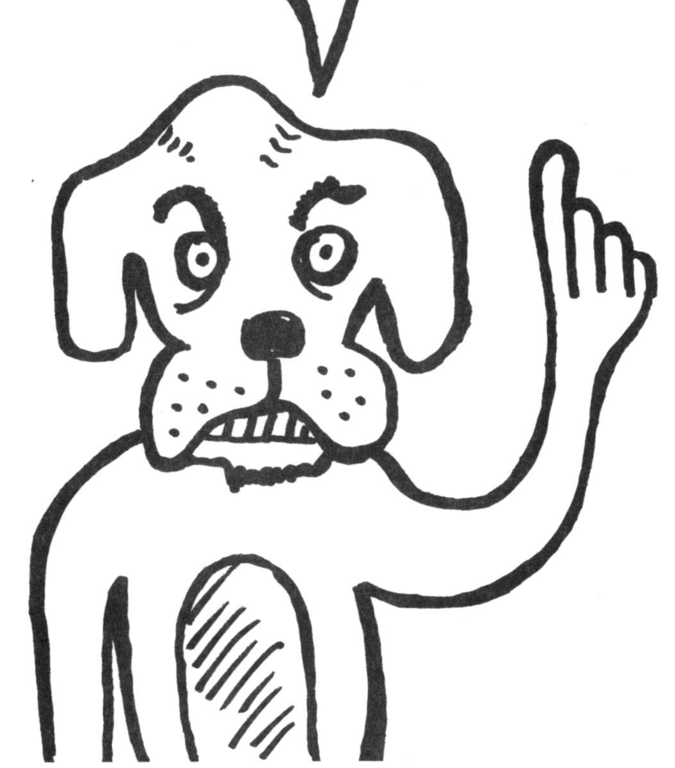
WISE MUTT SAY'S...
PUNK ROCK WAS LIKE EMERSON, LAKE AND PALMER'S FIRST ALBUM. IT WAS GOOD AT THE TIME.

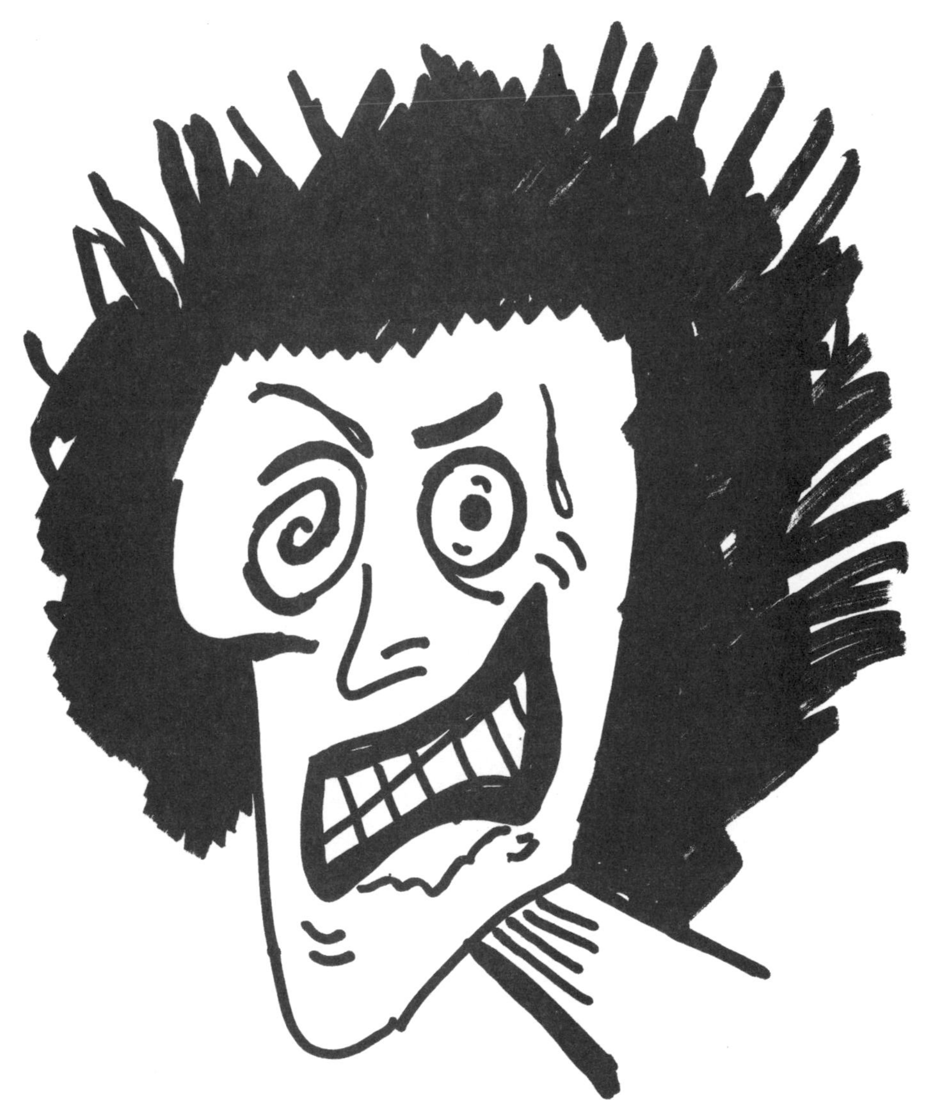

MEG THE MYSTIC

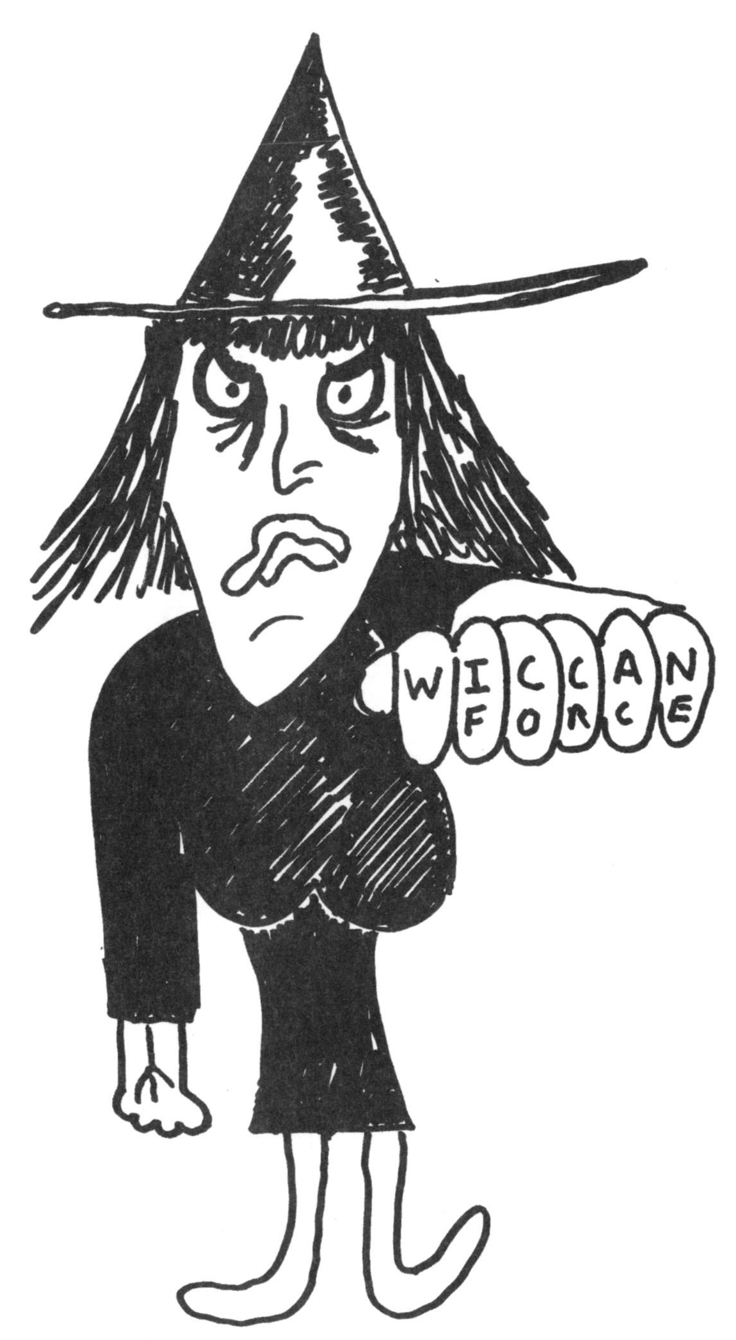
WICCAN
FORCE

WISE MUTT TALK'S ABOUT THE 60'S

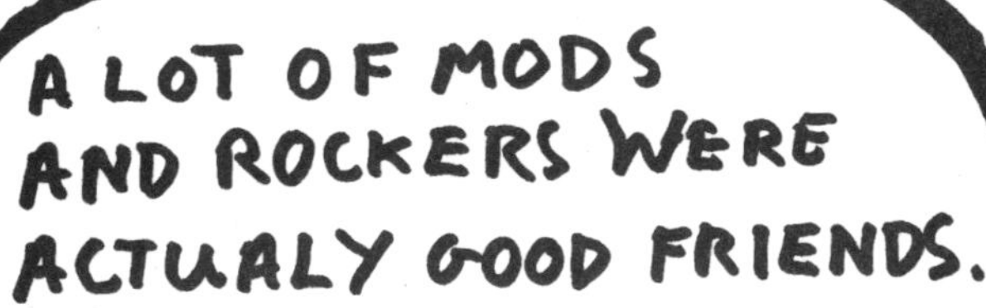

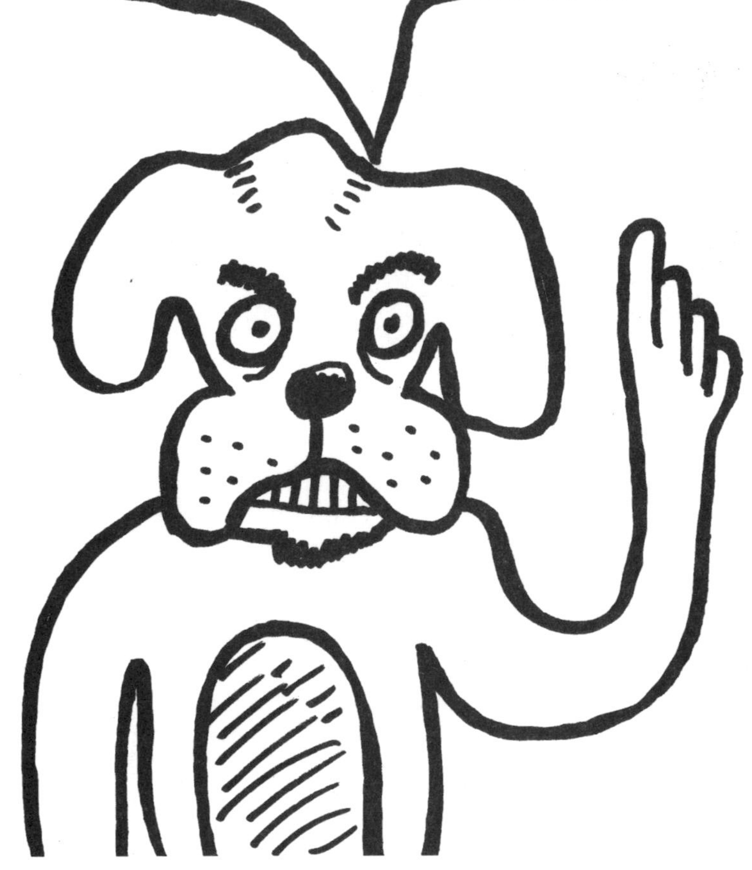

WISE MUTT SAYS...

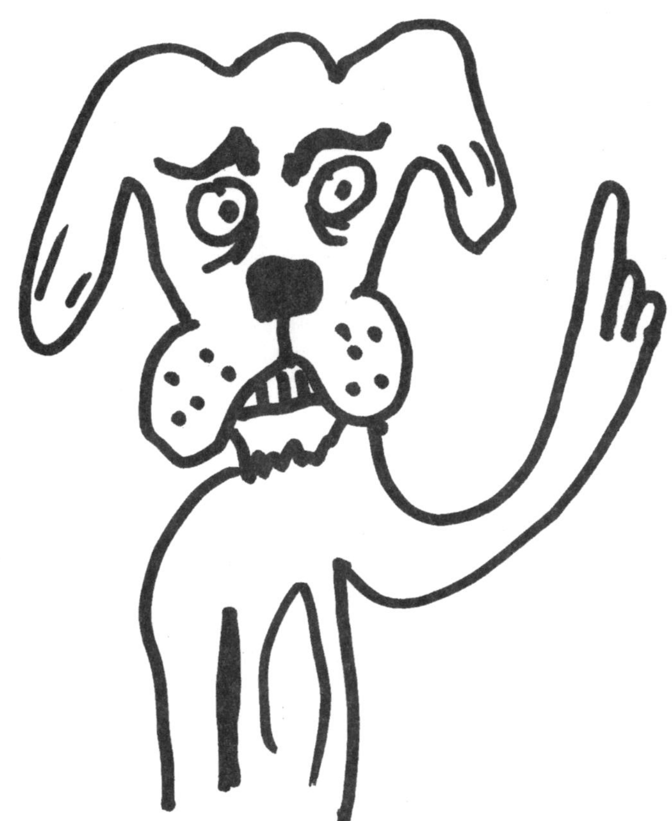

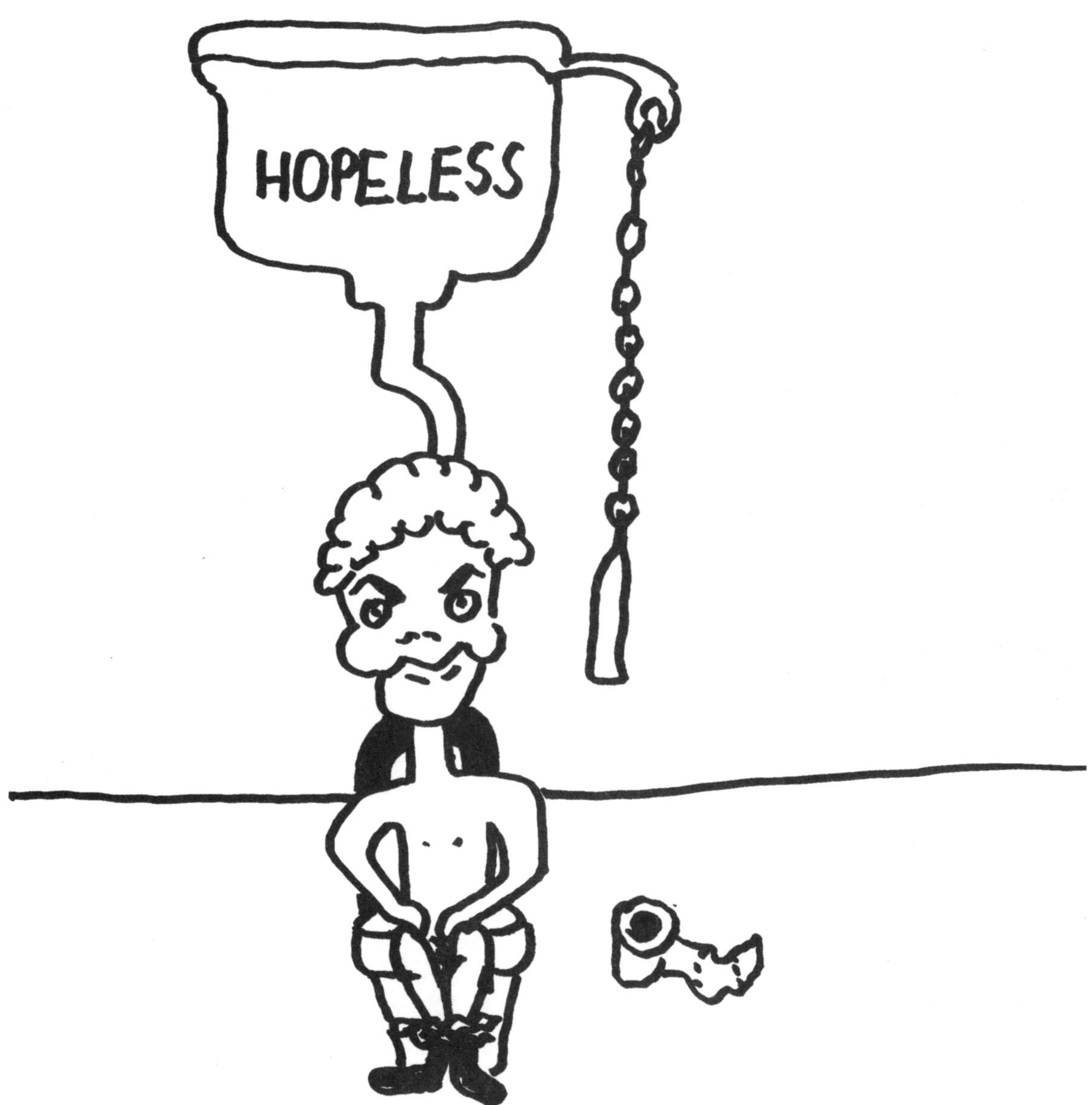
HOPELESS

PSYCHIATRIST AND NUT

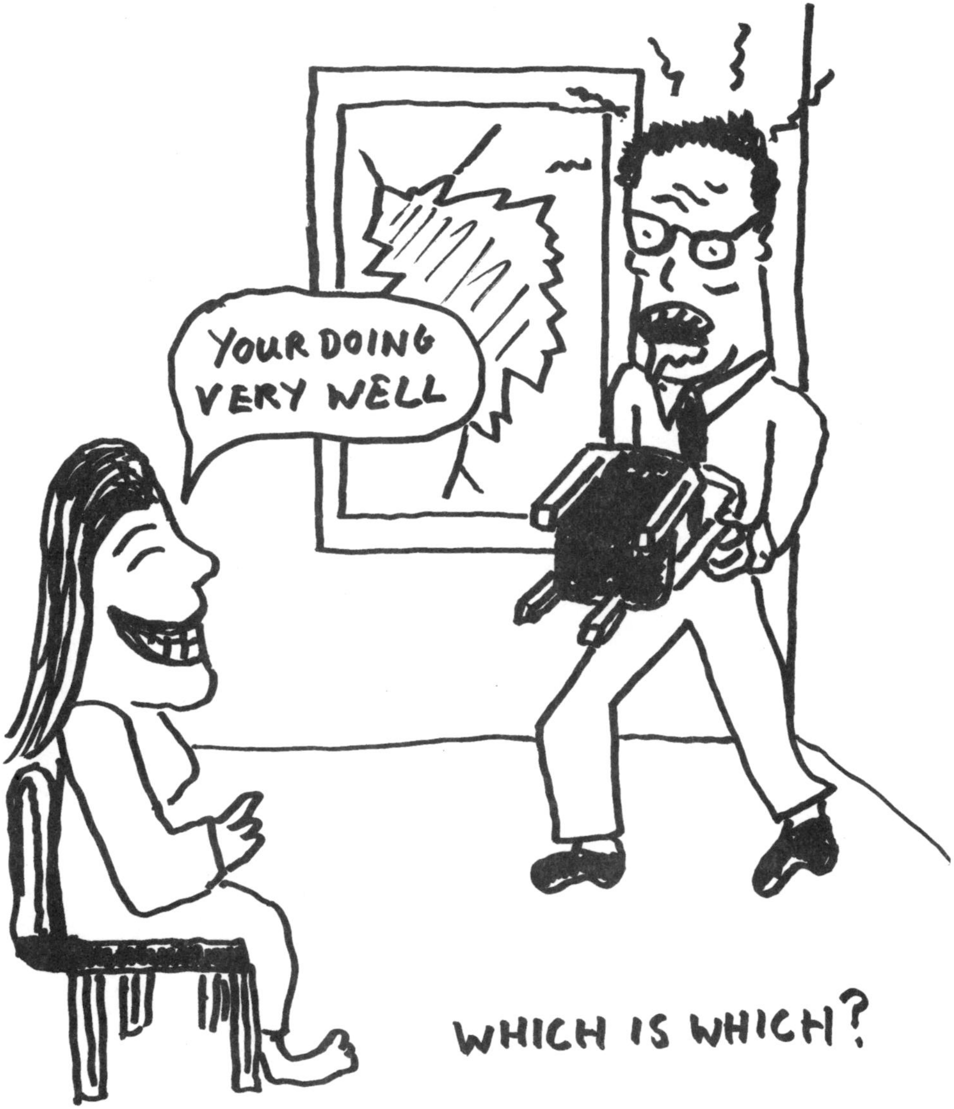

YOUR DOING
VERY WELL

WHICH IS WHICH?

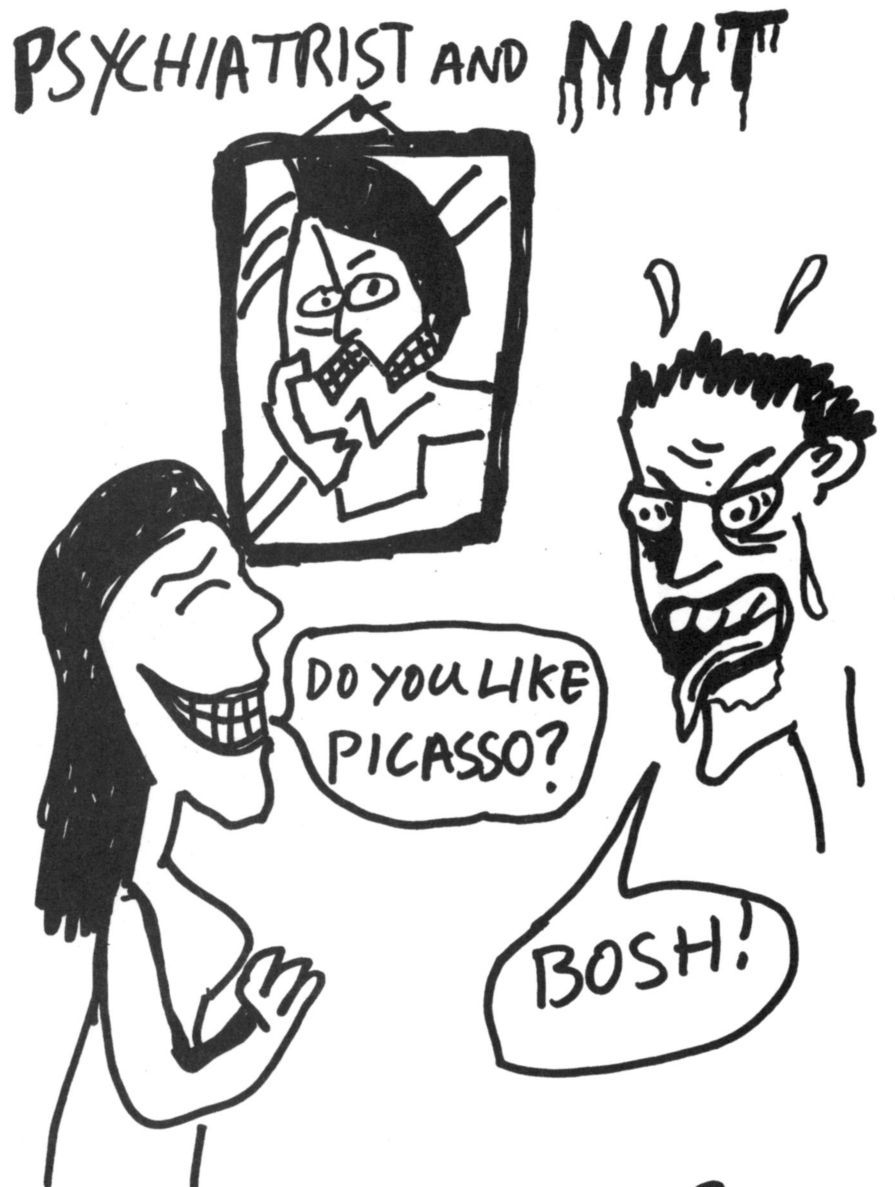

WHOT ONE'S WHOT?

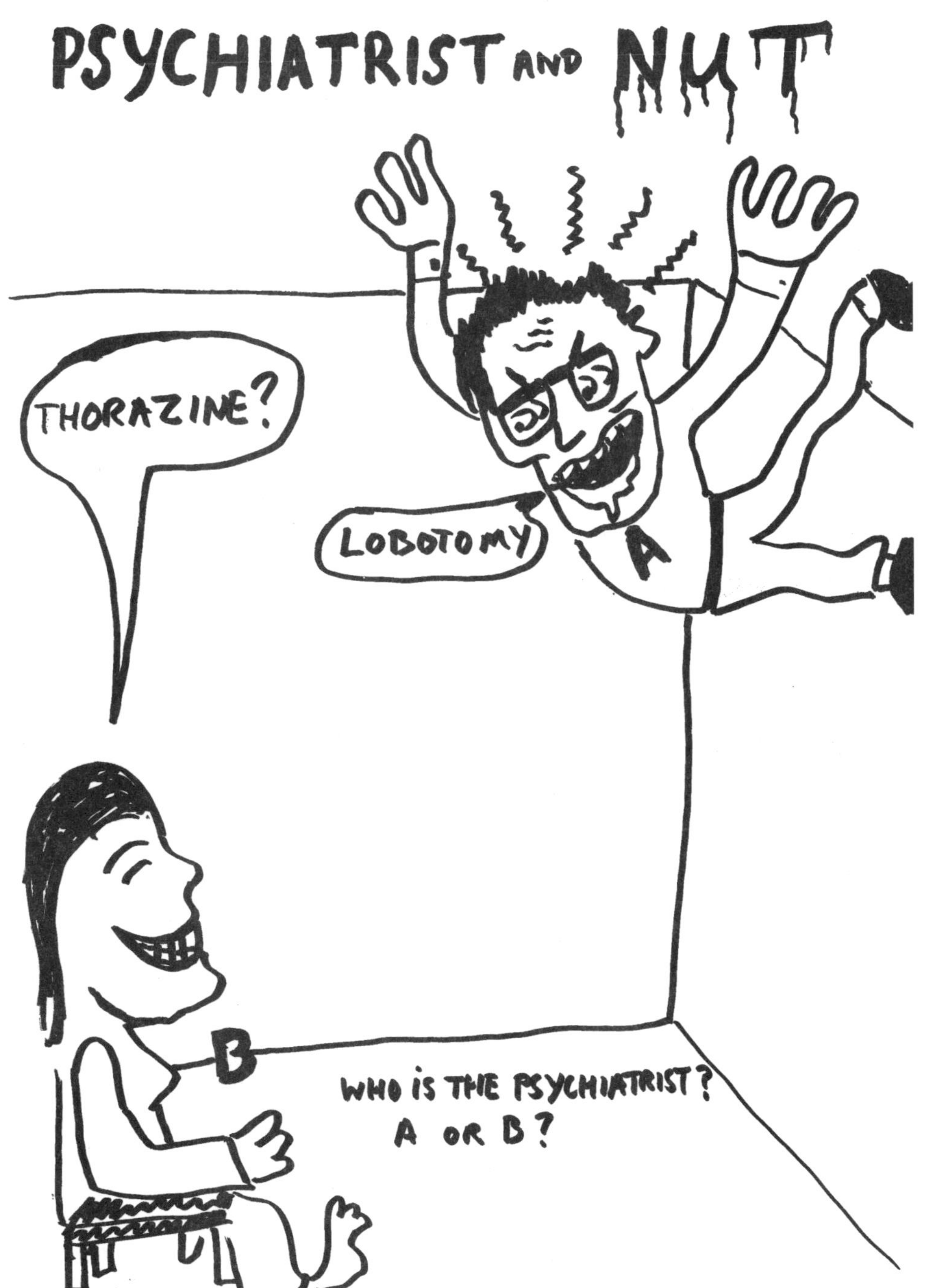
PSYCHIATRIST AND NUT
THORAZINE?
LOBOTOMY
A
B
WHO IS THE PSYCHIATRIST?
A OR B?

PSYCHIATRIST AND NUT

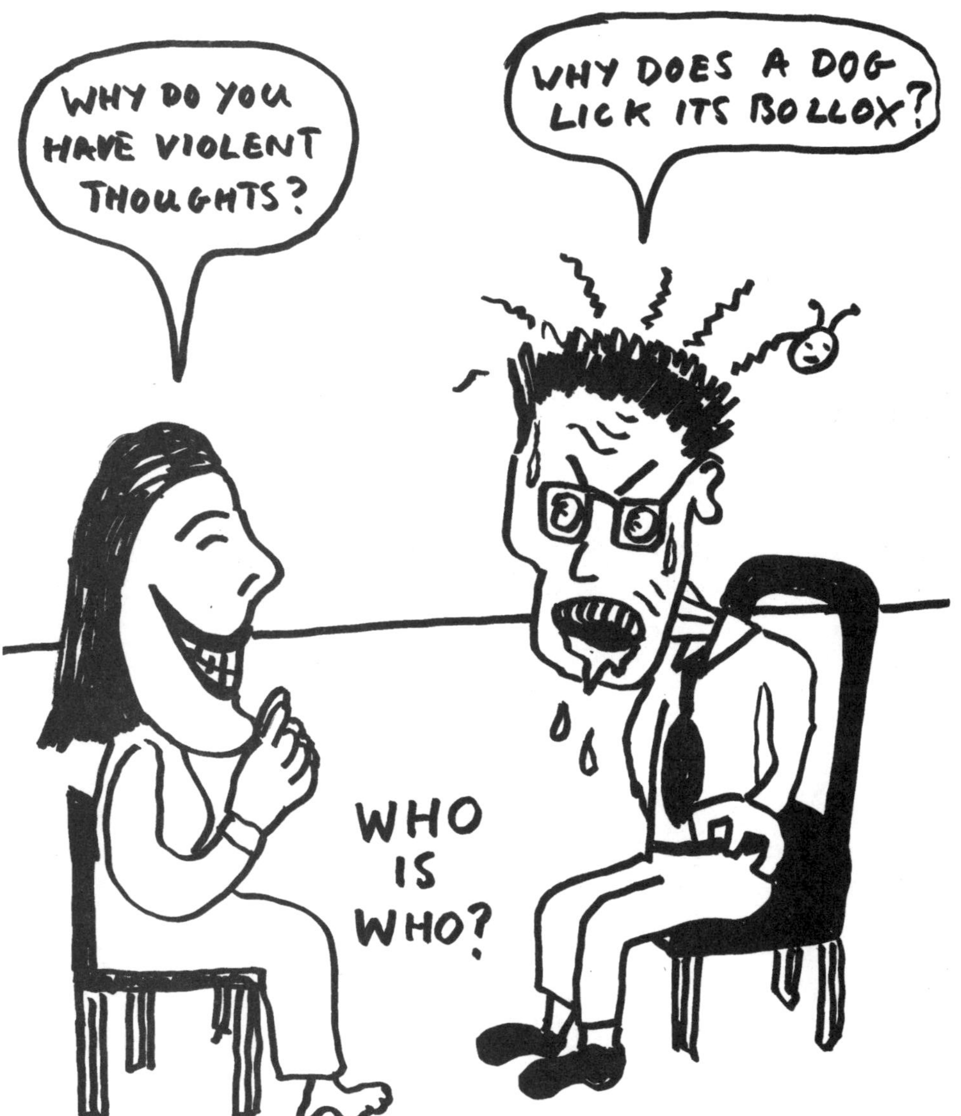

CONQUEST MOUSE

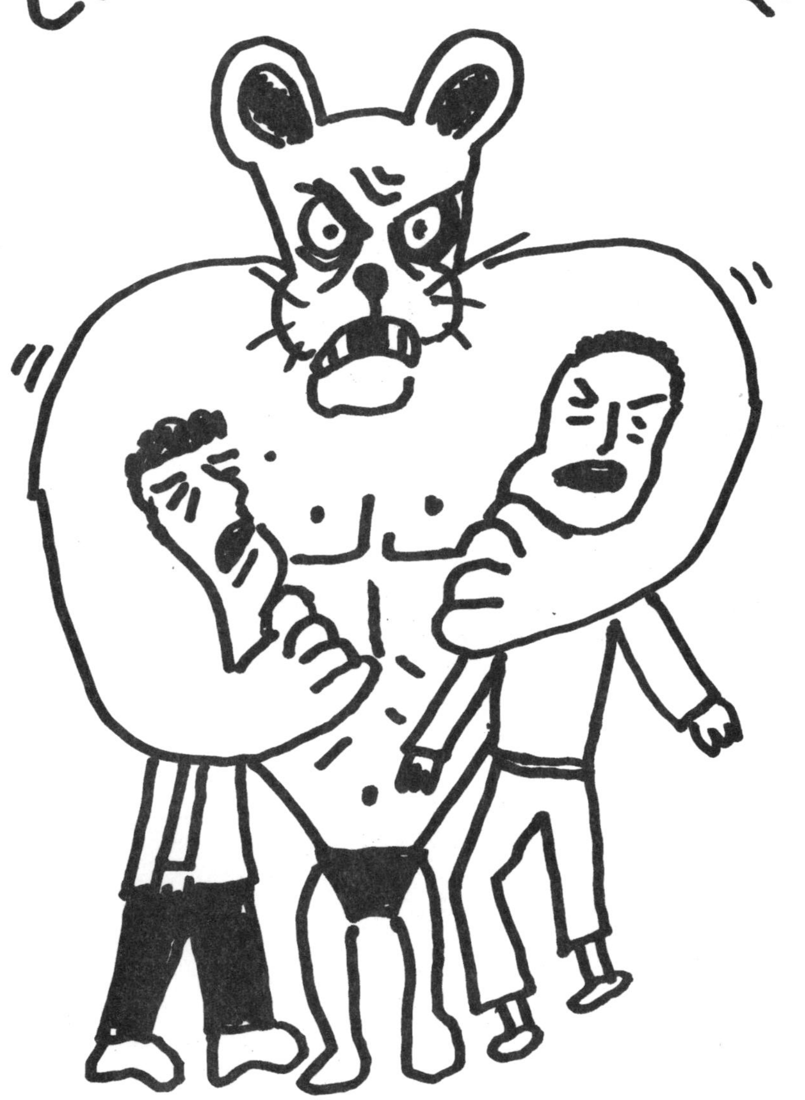

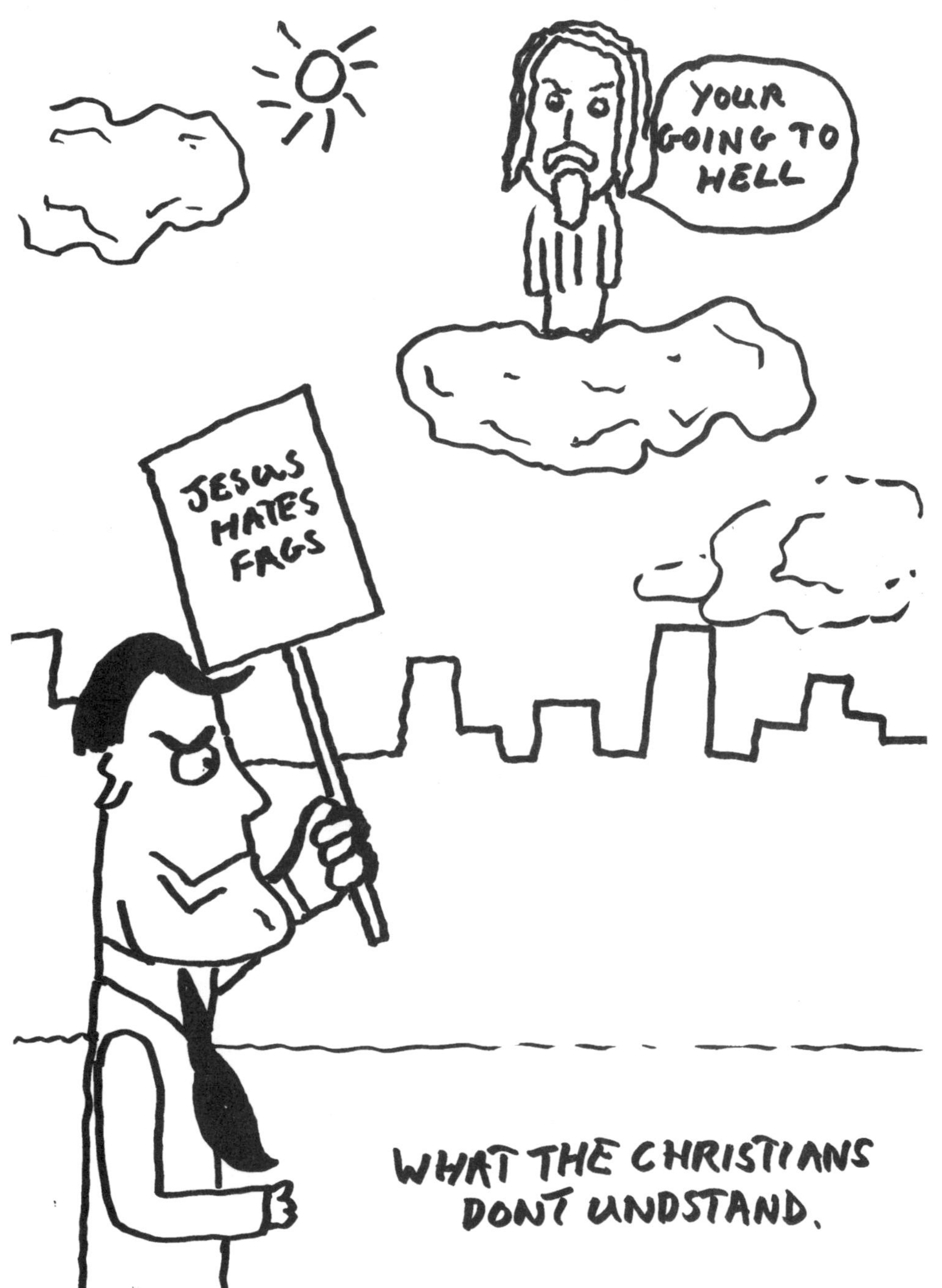

WHAT THE CHRISTIANS DONT UNDSTAND.

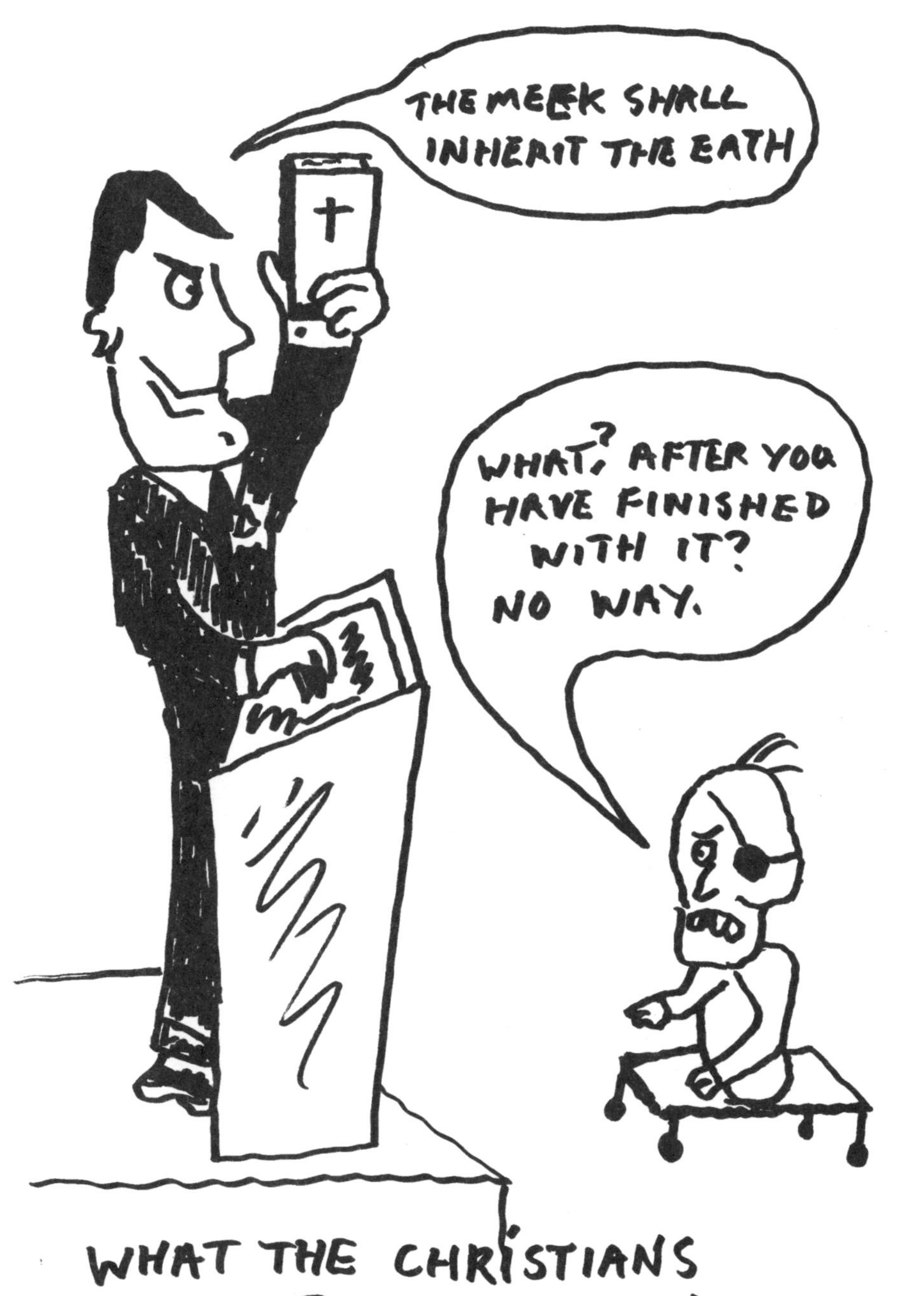

WHAT THE CHRISTIANS DONT UNDERSTAND

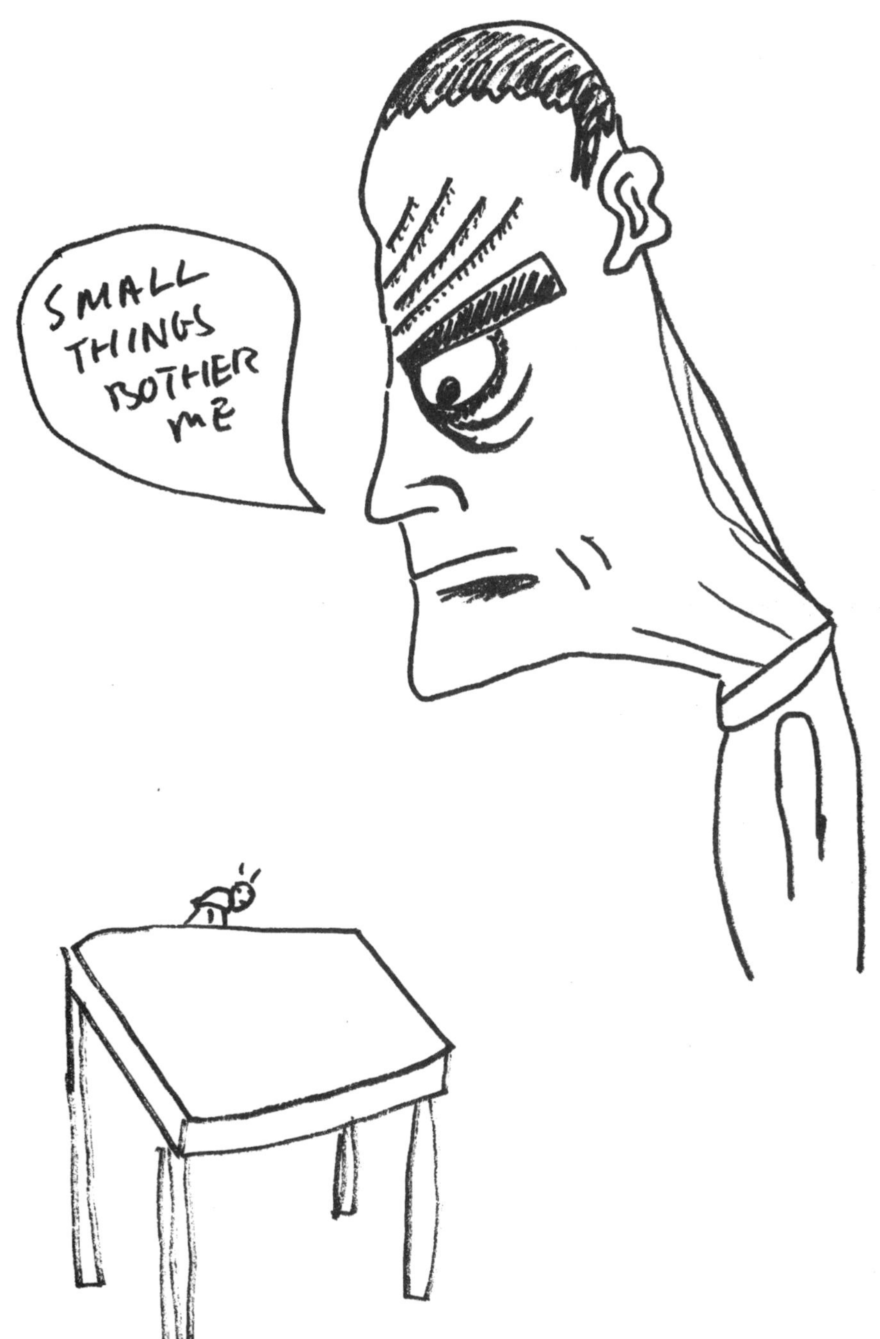
SMALL THINGS BOTHER ME

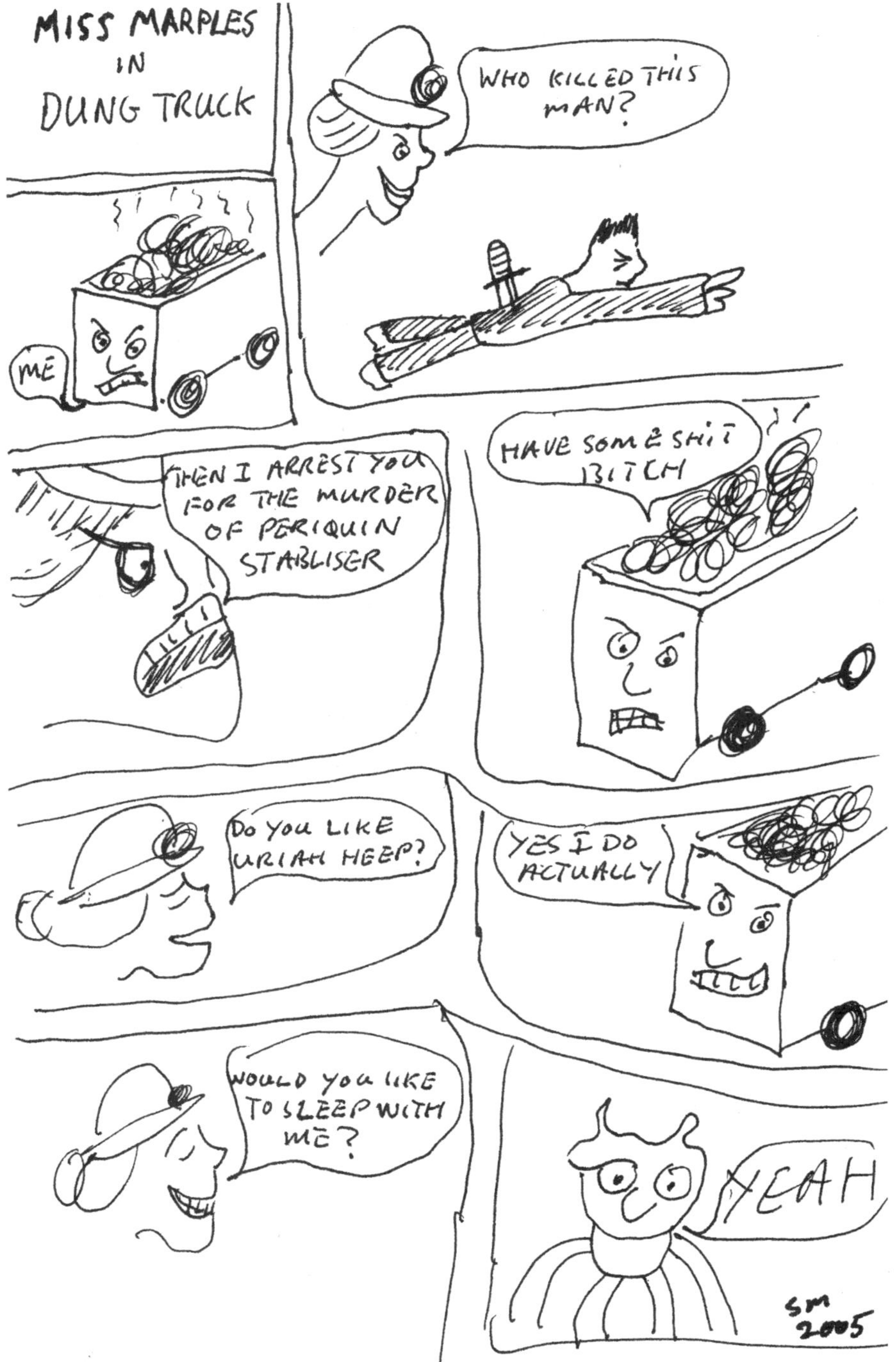
MISS MARPLES
IN
DUNG TRUCK
WHO KILLED THIS MAN?
ME
THEN I ARREST YOU FOR THE MURDER OF PERIQUIN STABLISER
HAVE SOME SHIT BITCH
DO YOU LIKE URIAH HEEP?
YES I DO ACTUALLY
WOULD YOU LIKE TO SLEEP WITH ME?
YEAH
SM
2005

ANGRY PEOPLE

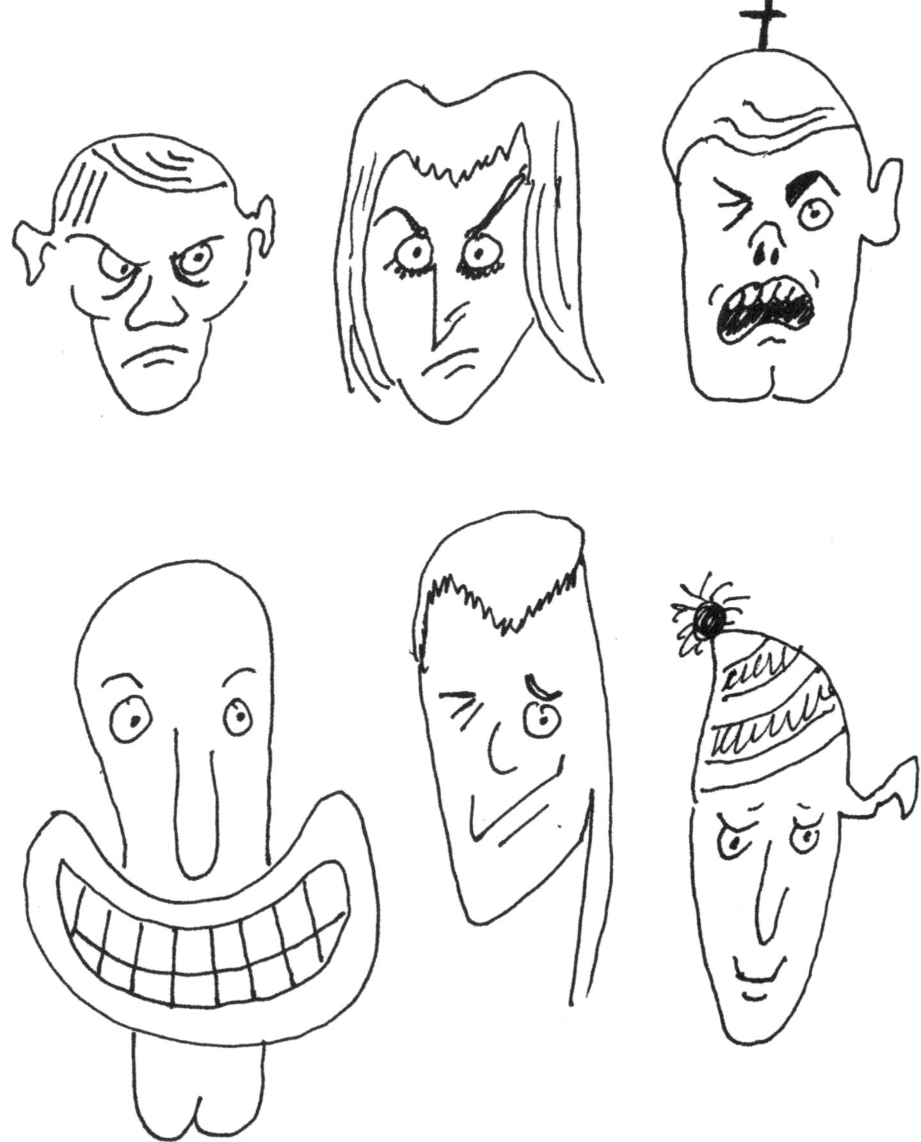

HAPPY PEOPLE

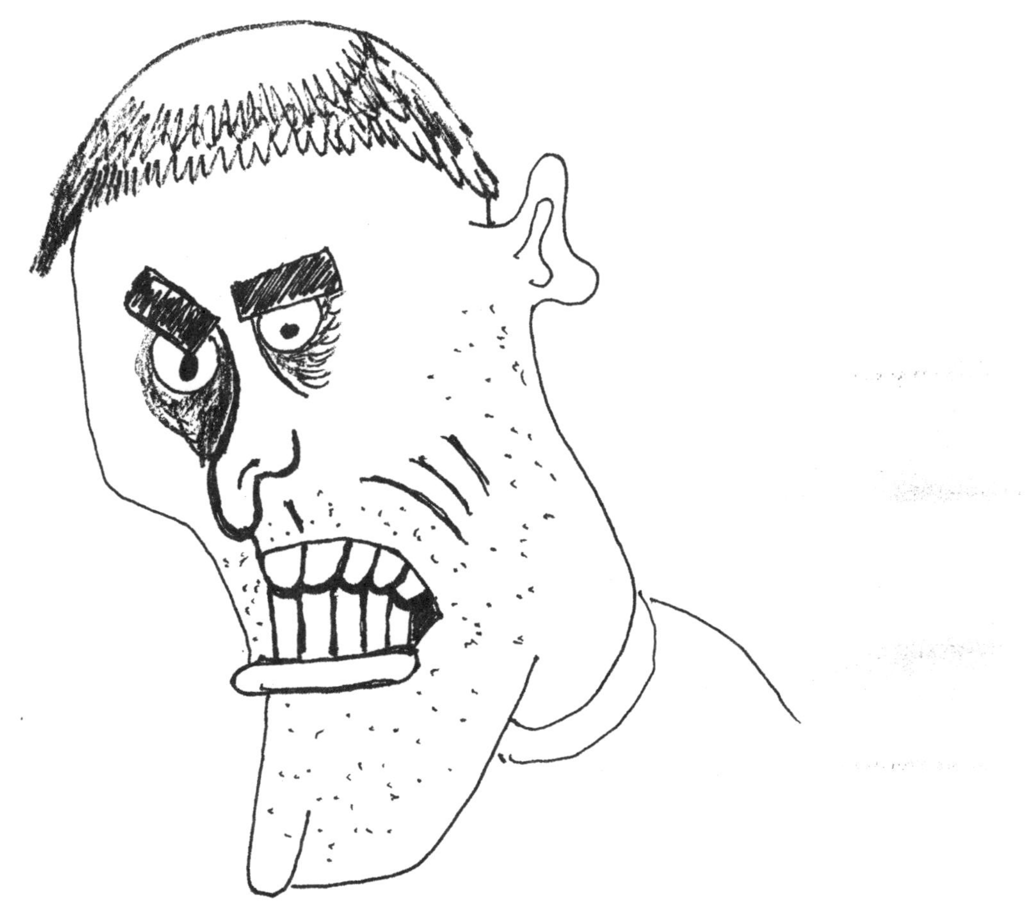

TYRENT
MONK

BOLLOCK CHOPS

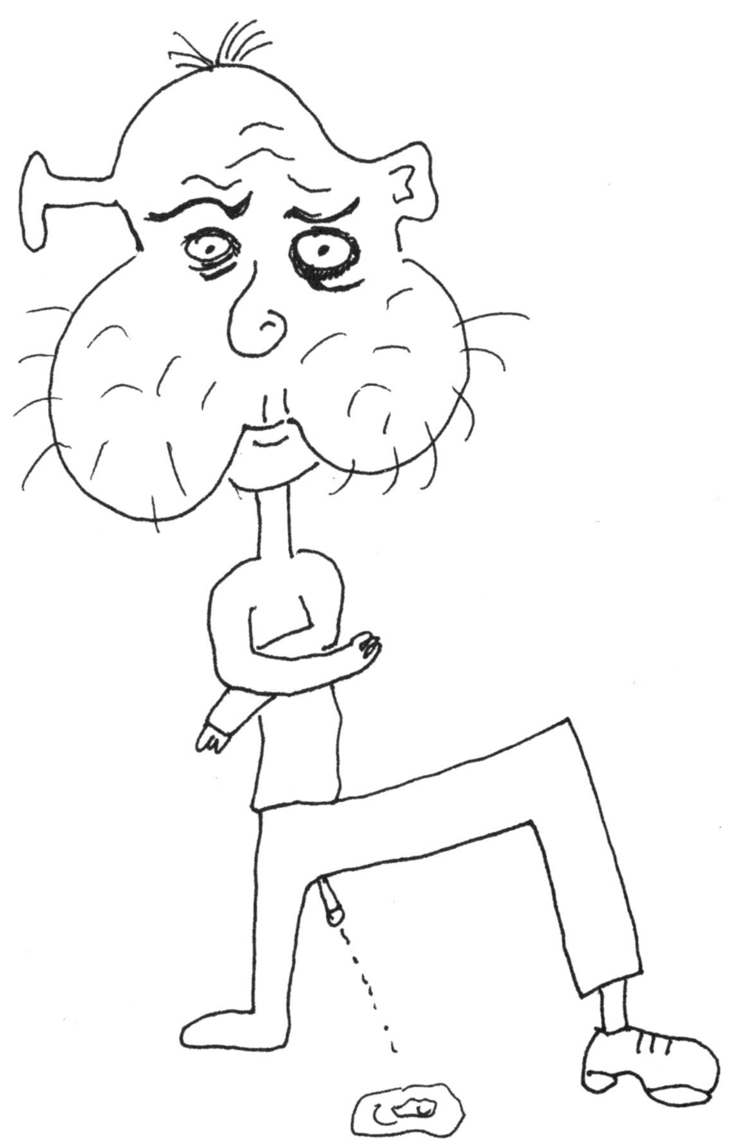

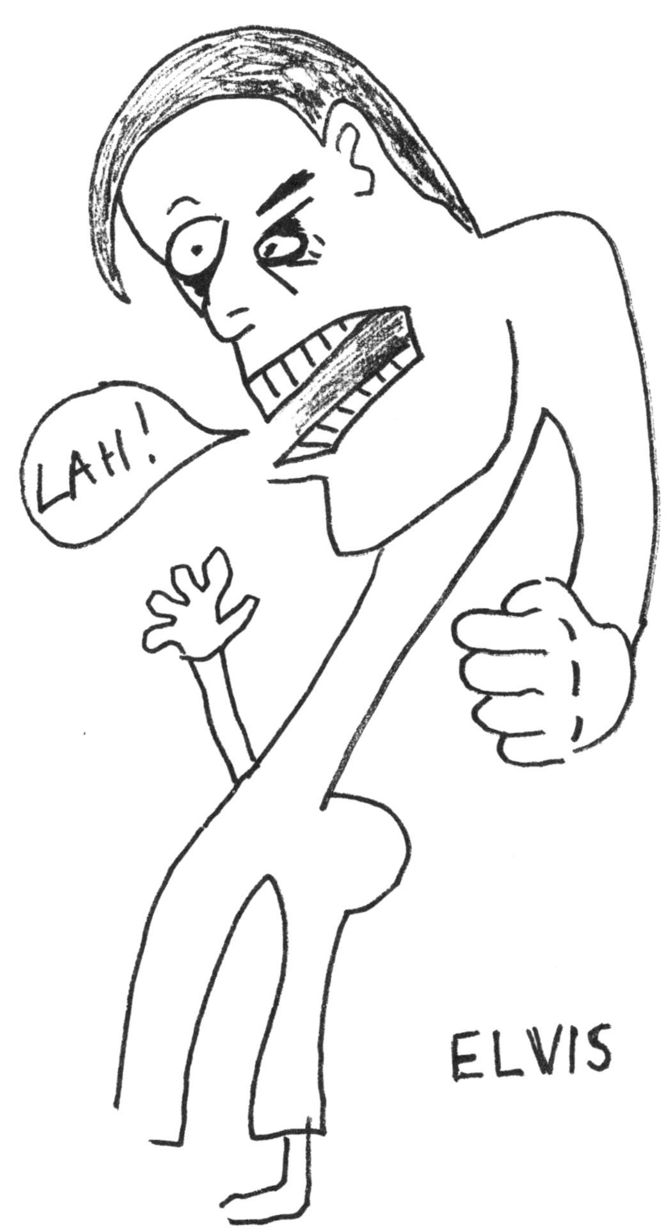
LAH!
ELVIS

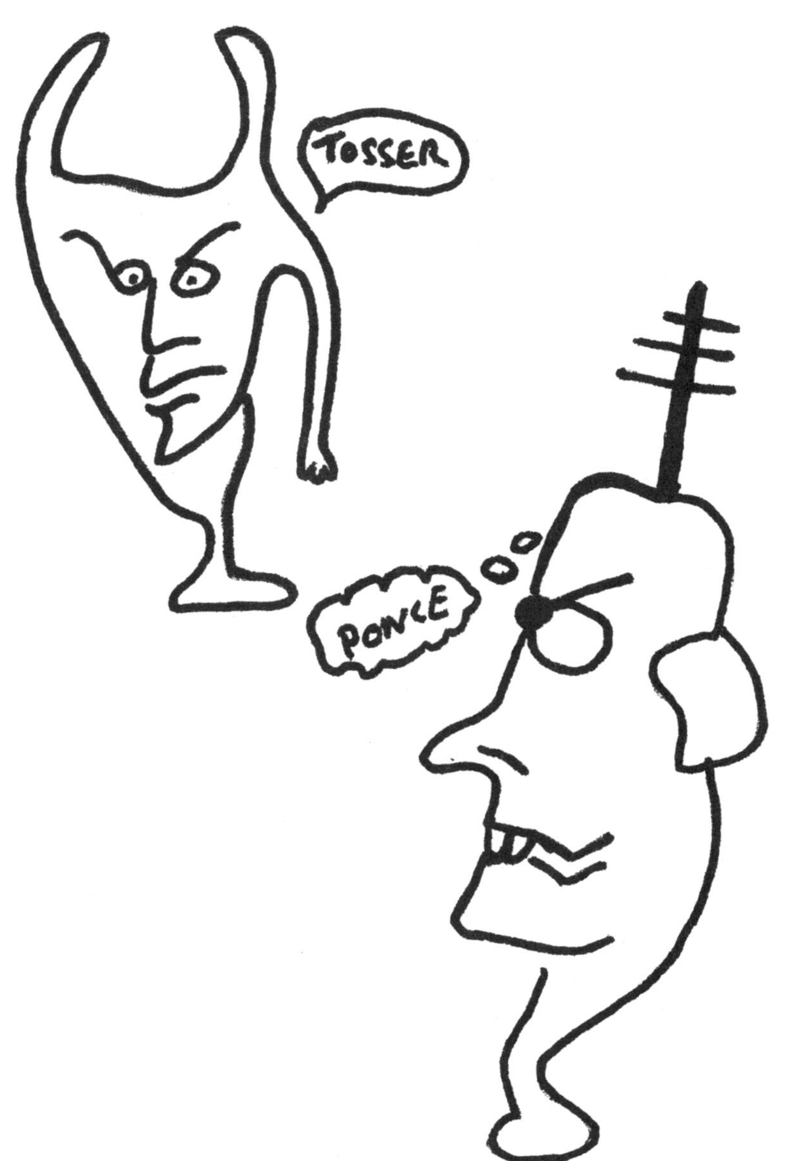
TOSSER
PONCE

WISE MUTT SAYS...

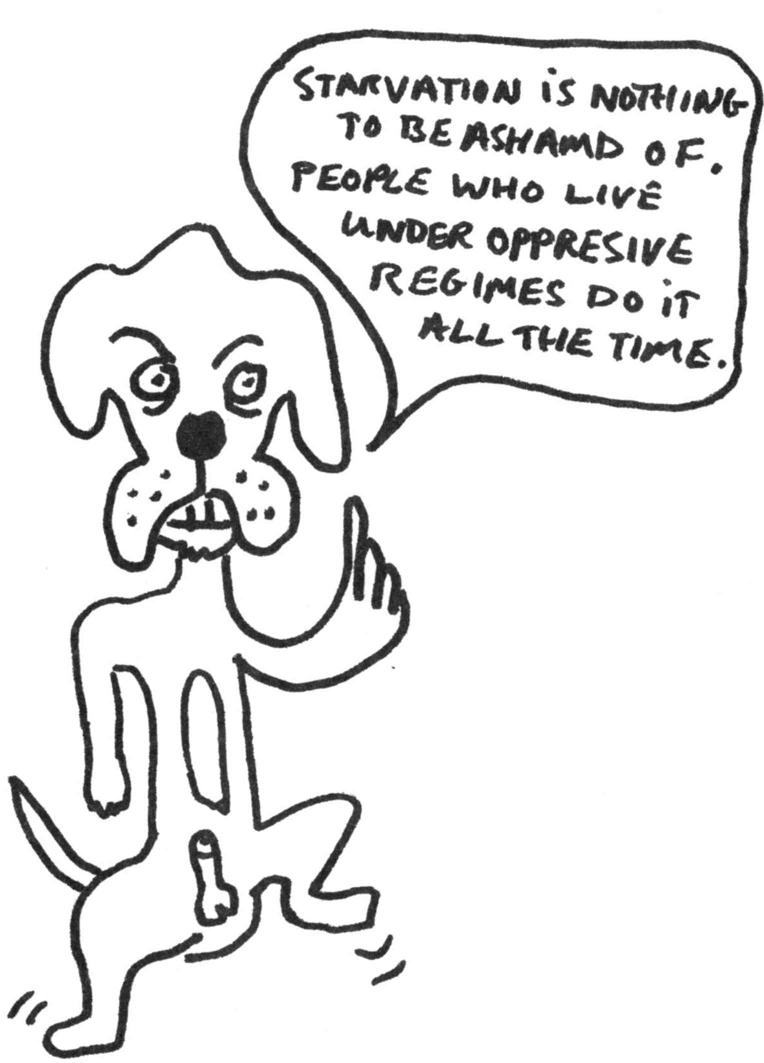

CHILD OF THE UNIVERSE

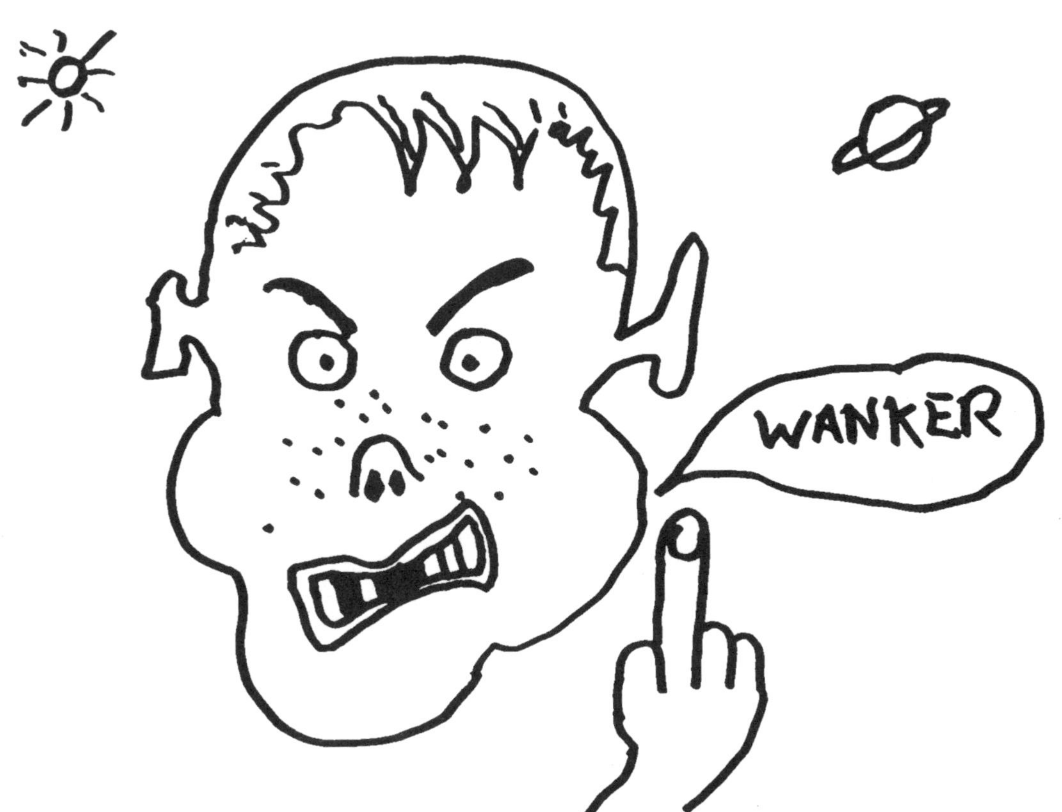

YOU HAVE A RIGHT TO BE HERE

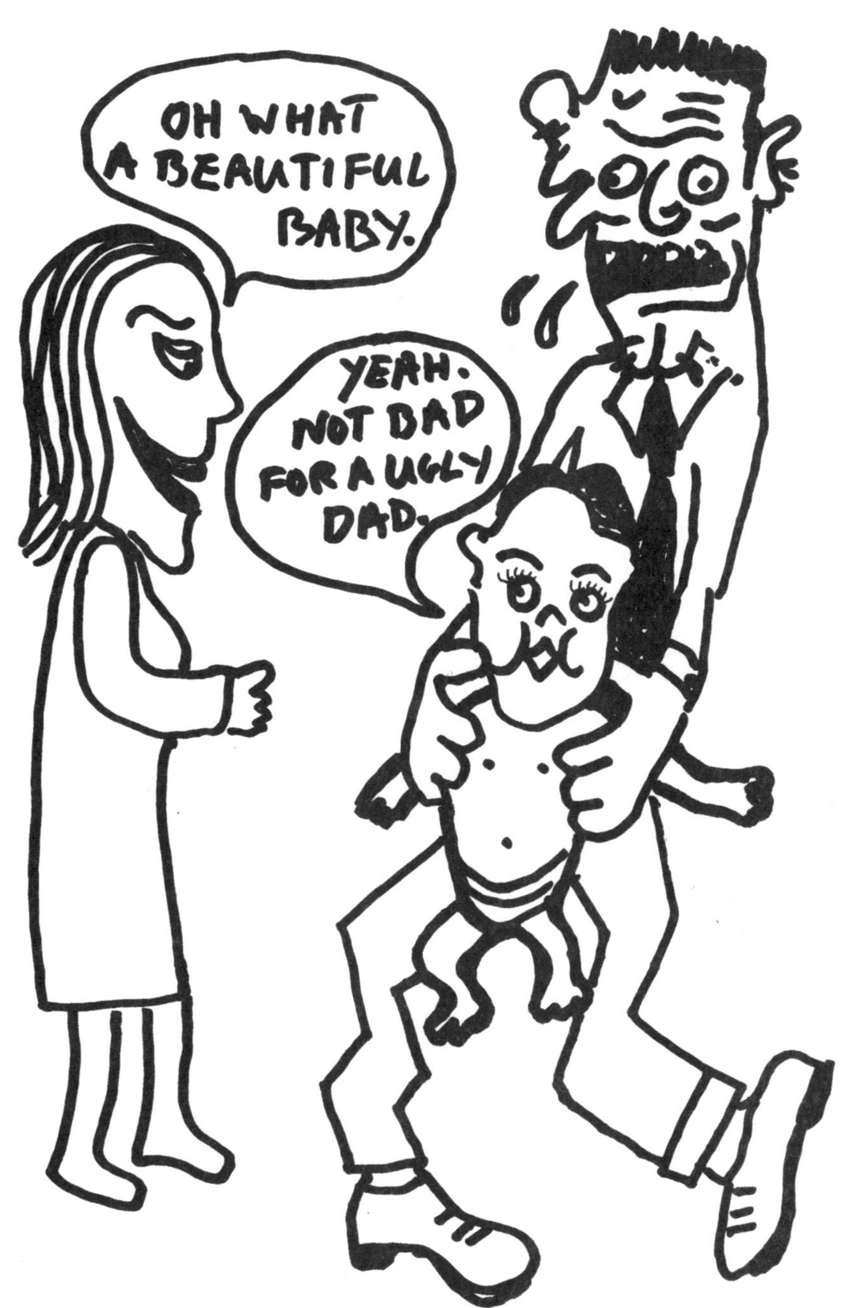
OH WHAT A BEAUTIFUL BABY.
YEAH. NOT BAD FOR A UGLY DAD.

SINISTER MUM

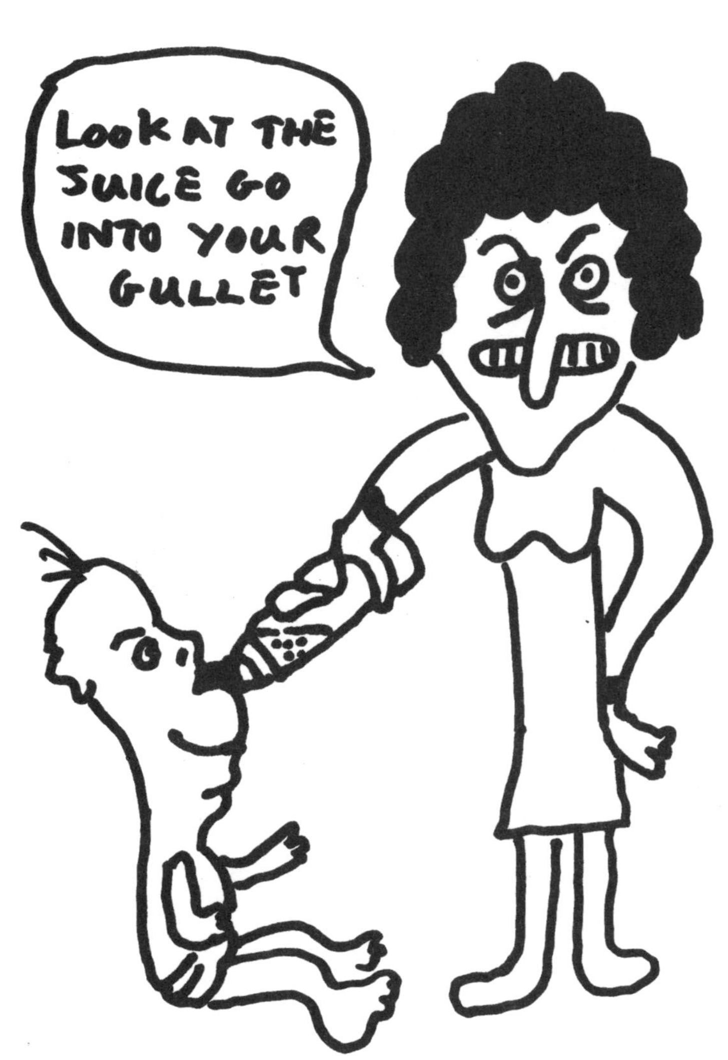

SINISTER MUM

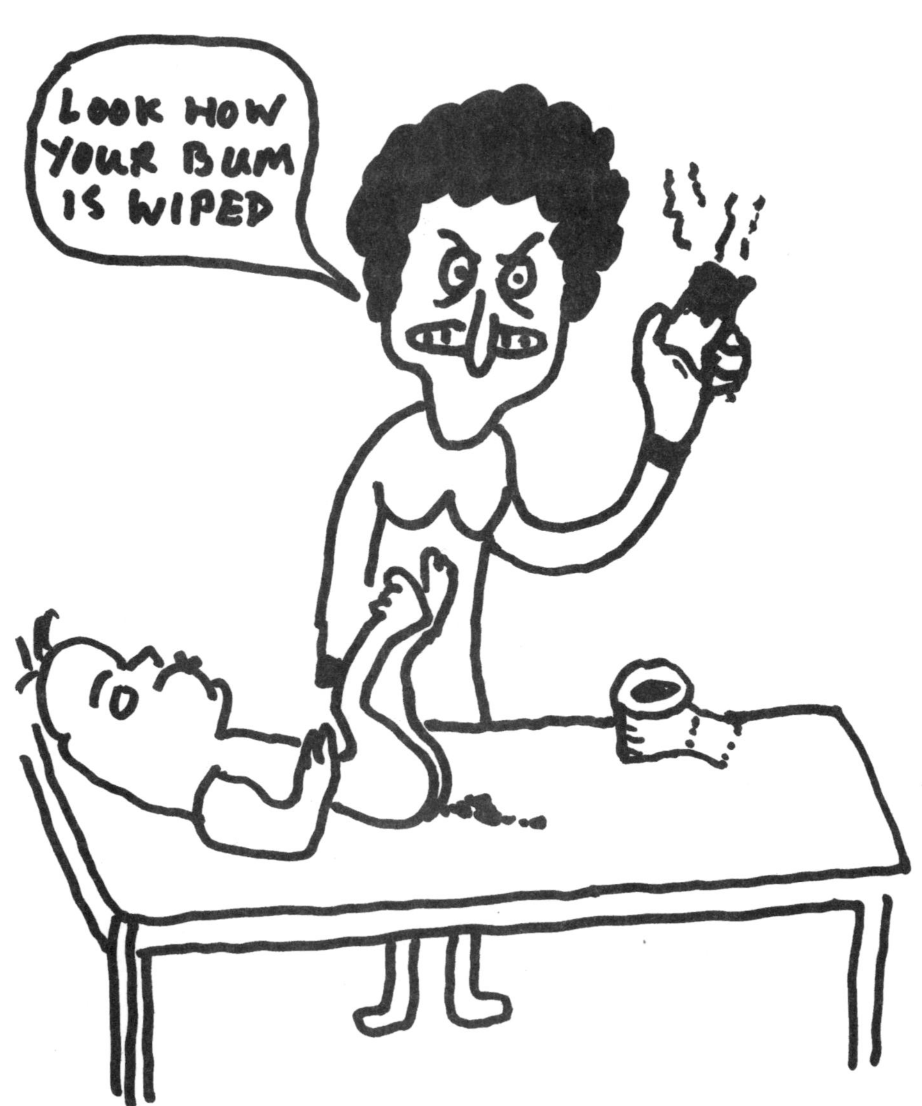

WISE MUTT SAYS...

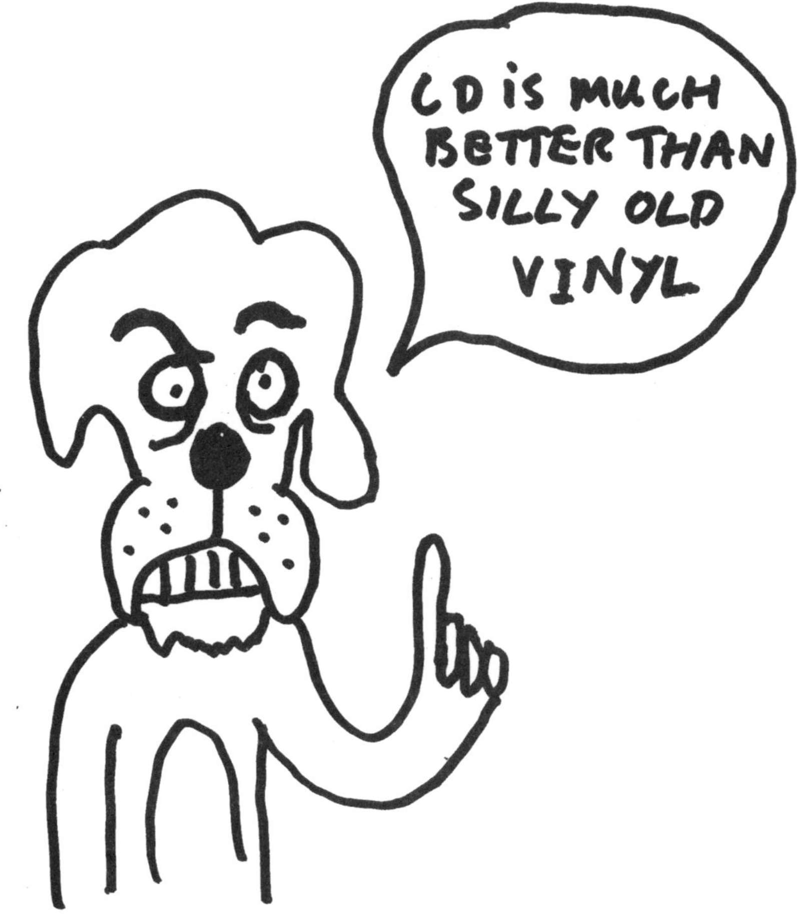

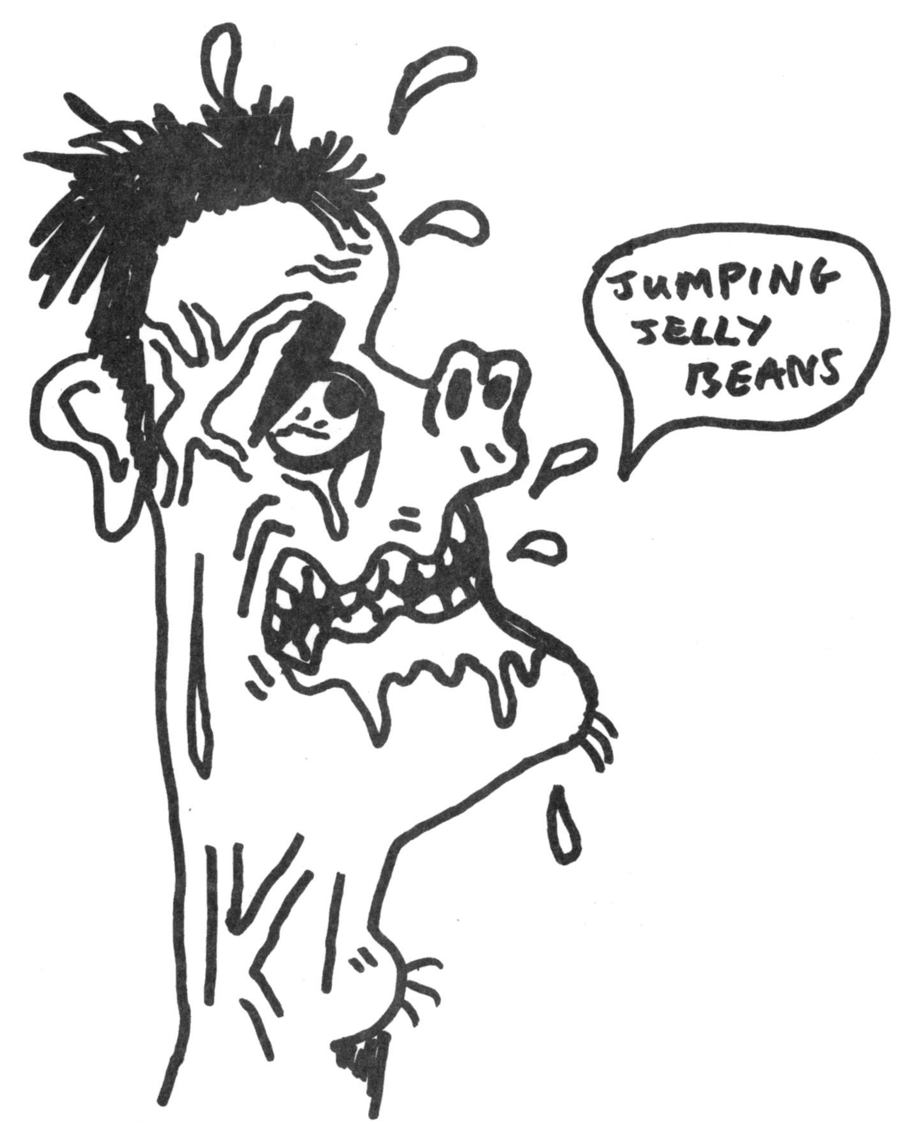

MAN HAVING HIS BALLS SQUEEZED (SLOWLY)

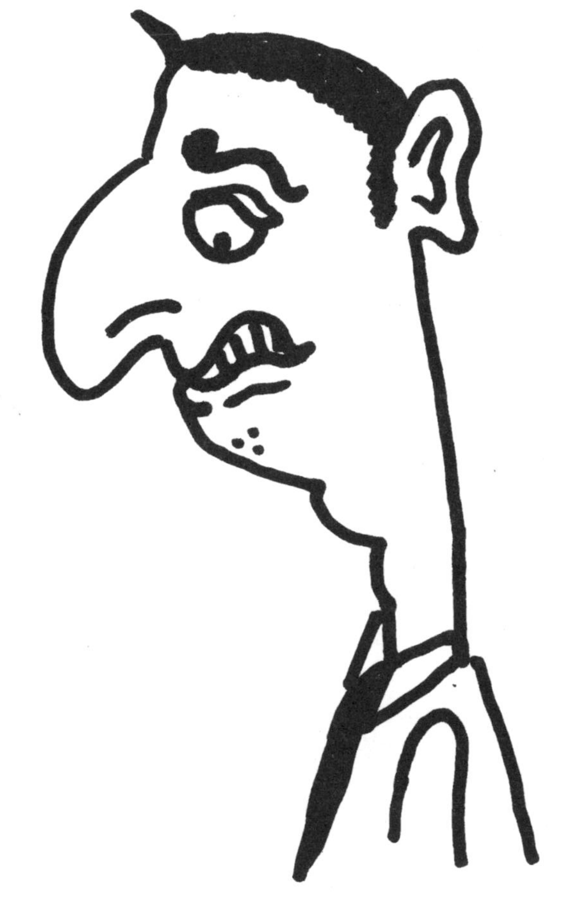

PRATT FACE.
THE CHINLESS WONDER.

ITS FRIDAY!

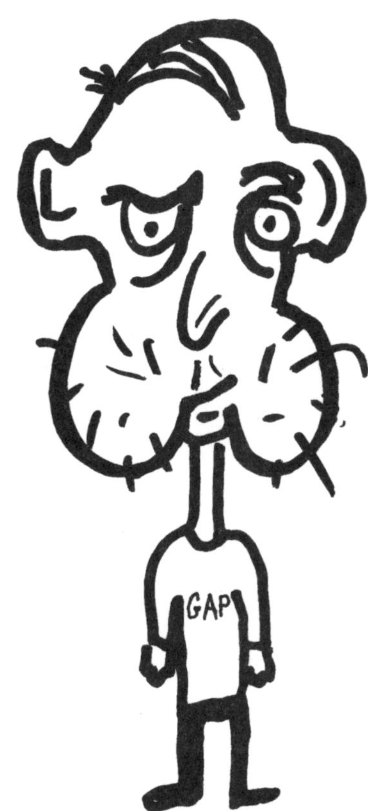

ITS BOLLOCK CHOPS!

DOMINANT BABY

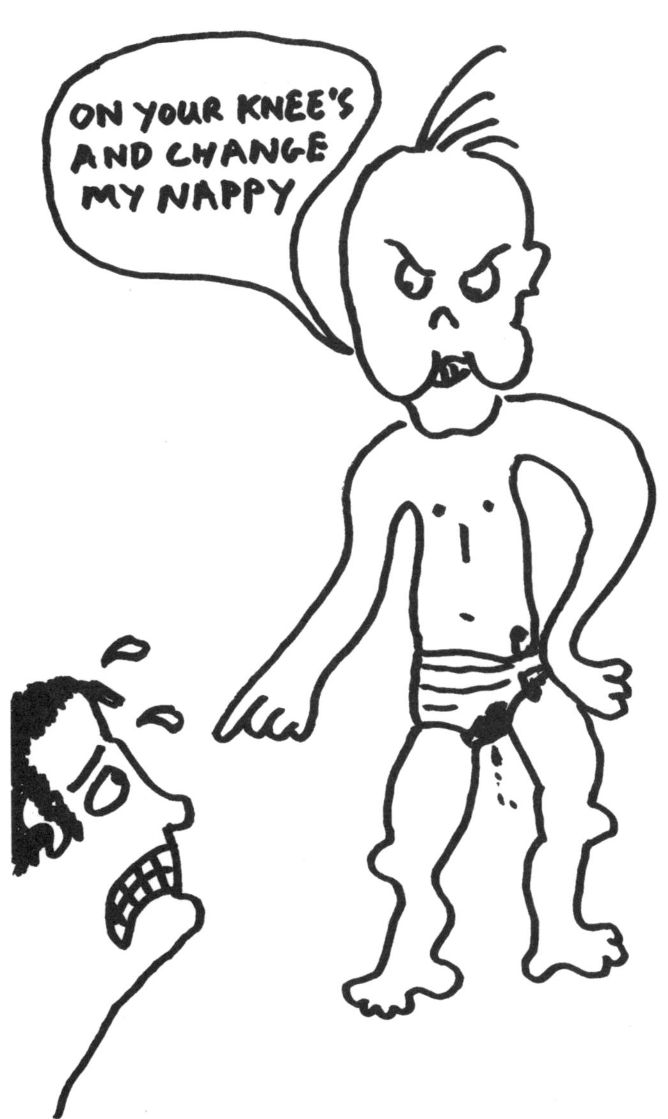

DOMINANT BABY

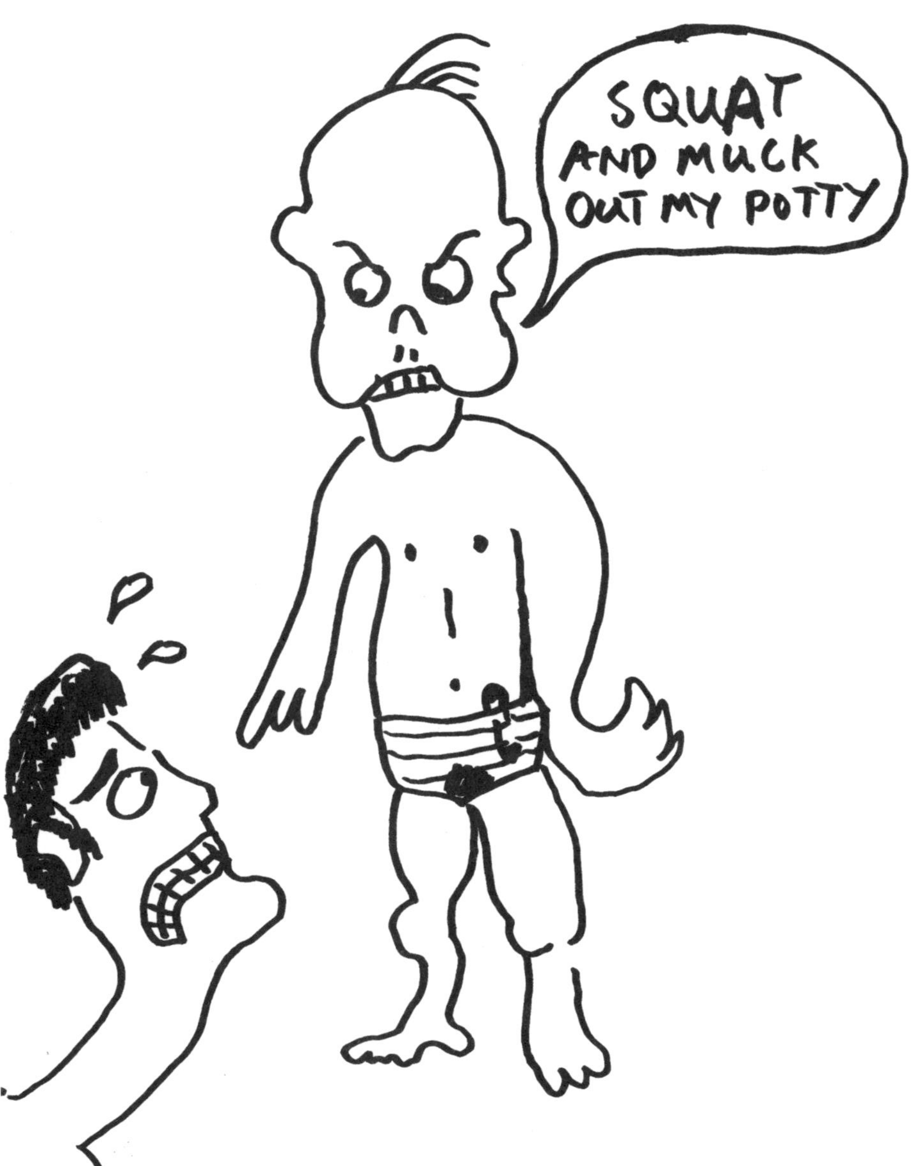

DOMINANT BABY

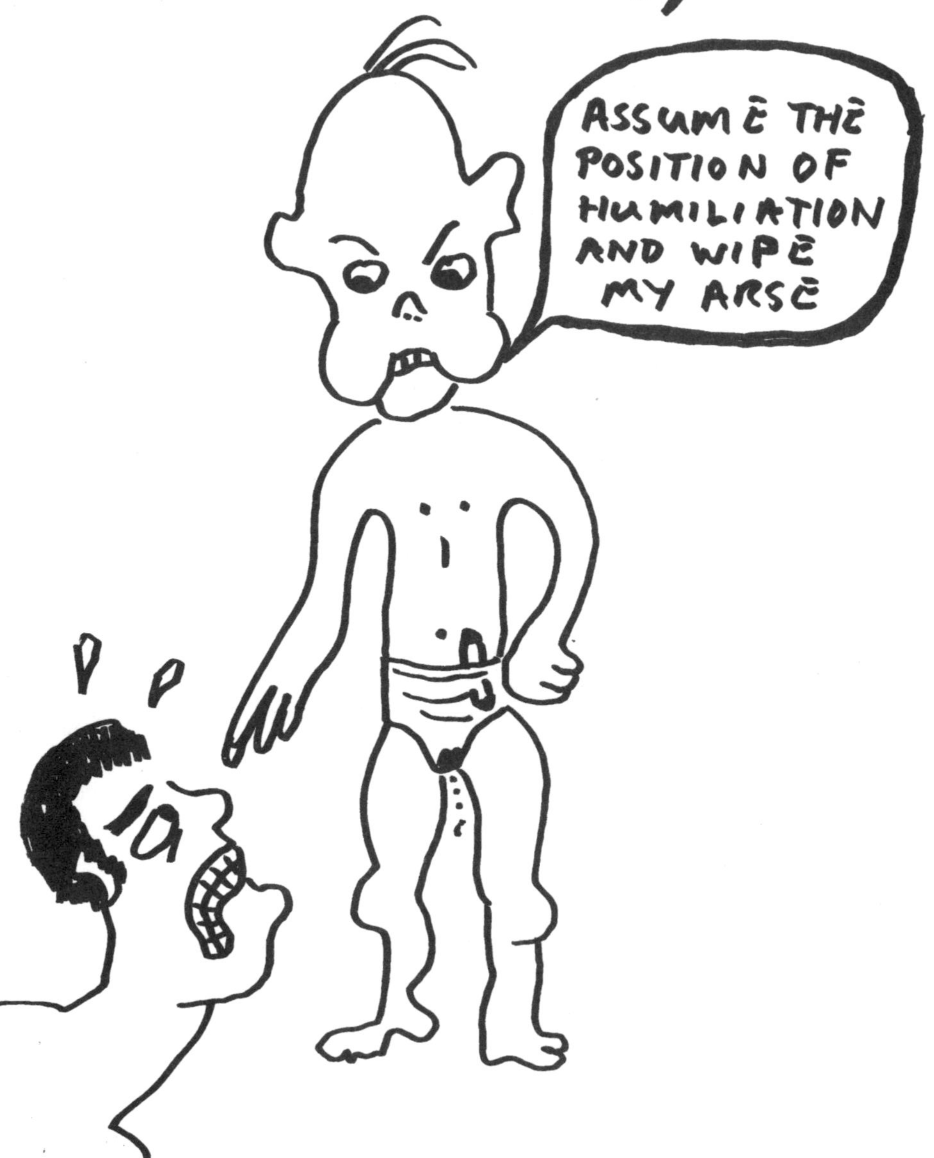

DOMINANT BABY

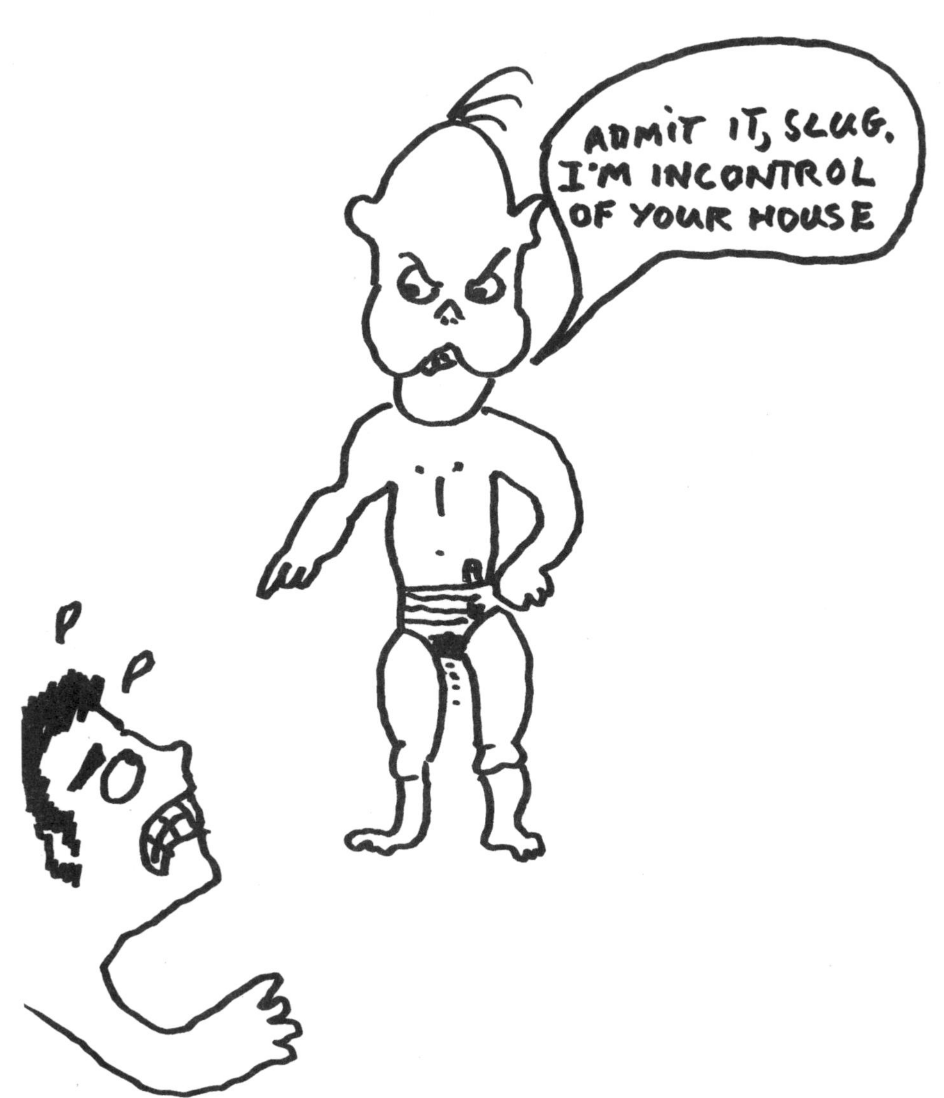

TRANSVESTITES IN POLOTIC'S

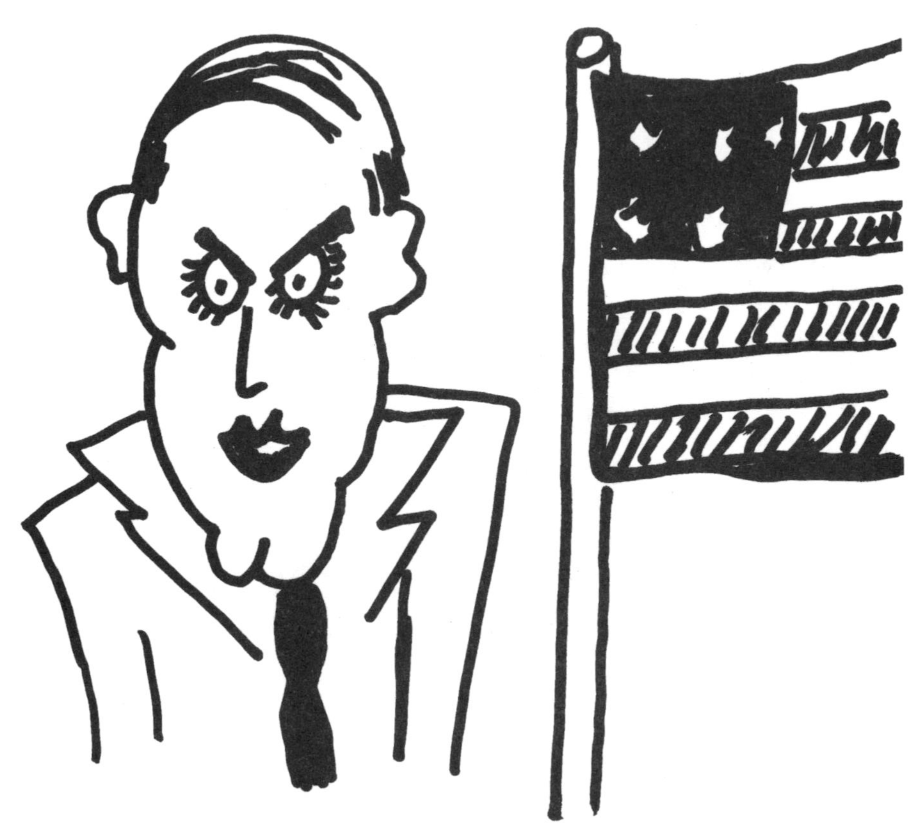

NO 1: EDGER J. HOOVER.

VIOLENT CHESHIRE CAT

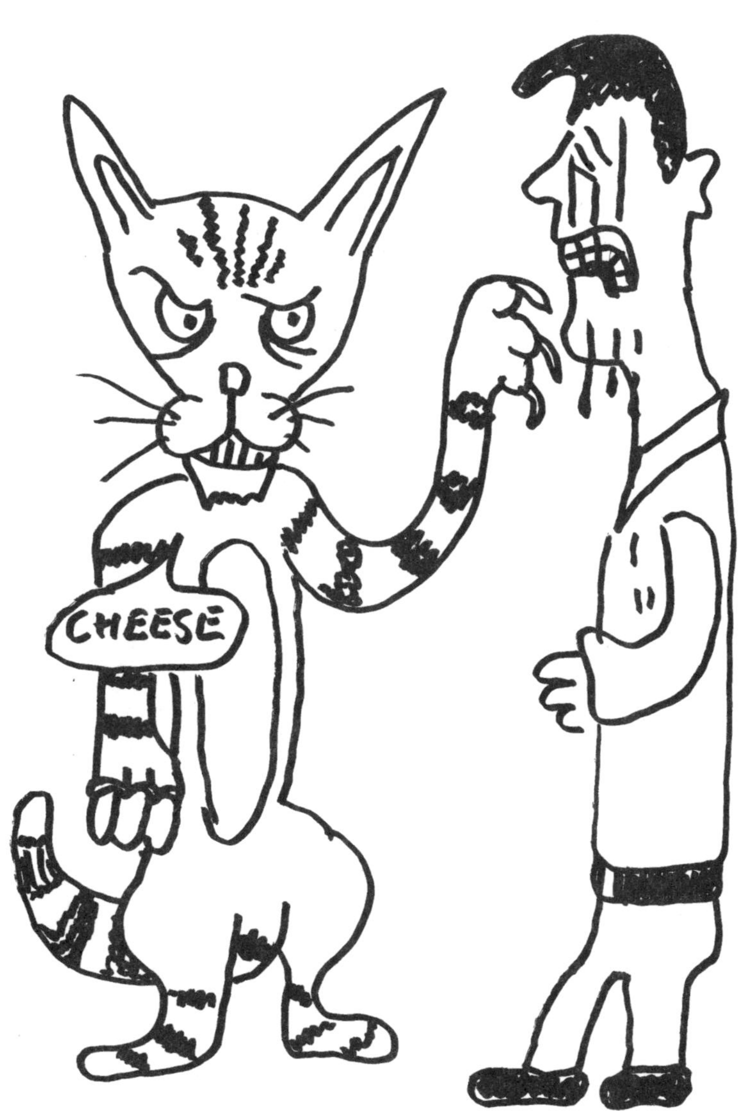

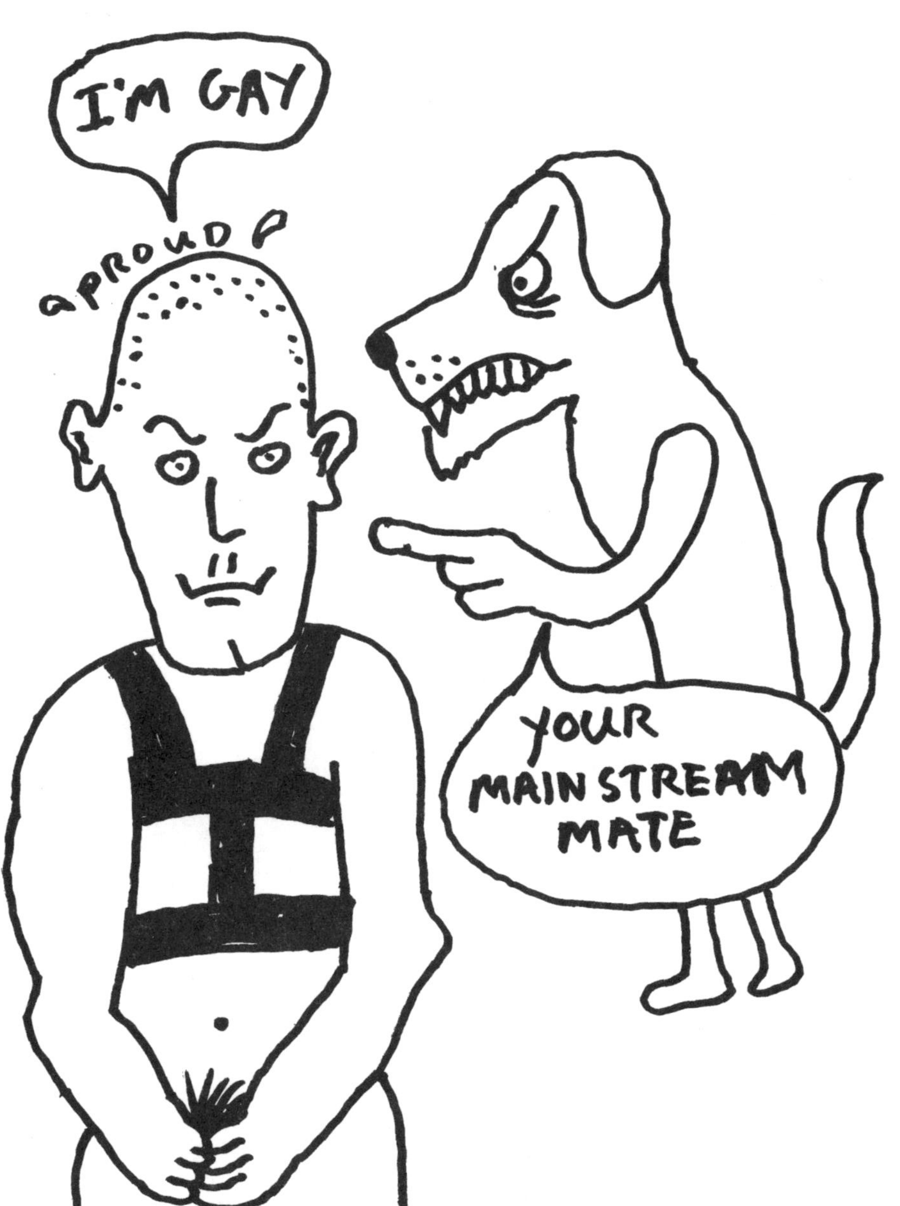
I'M GAY
a PROUD
YOUR MAINSTREAM MATE

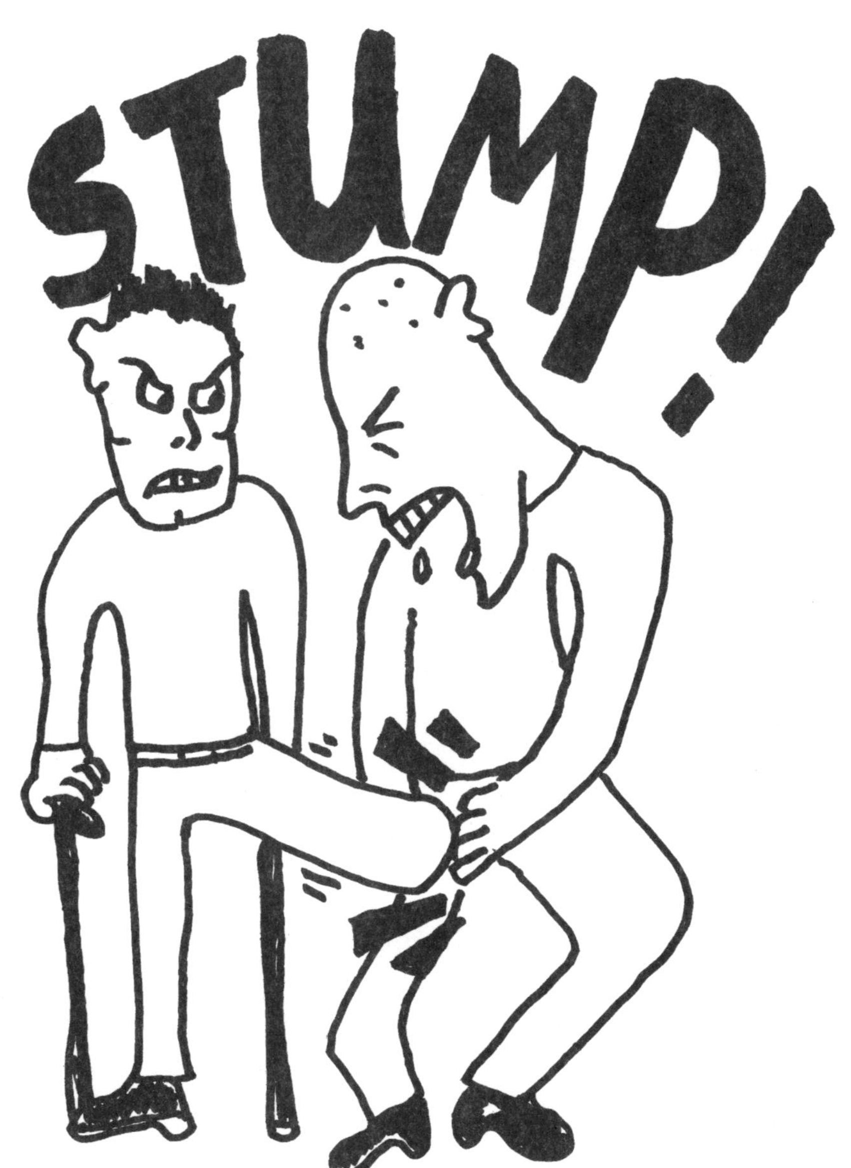
STUMP!

WISE MUTT SAYS...

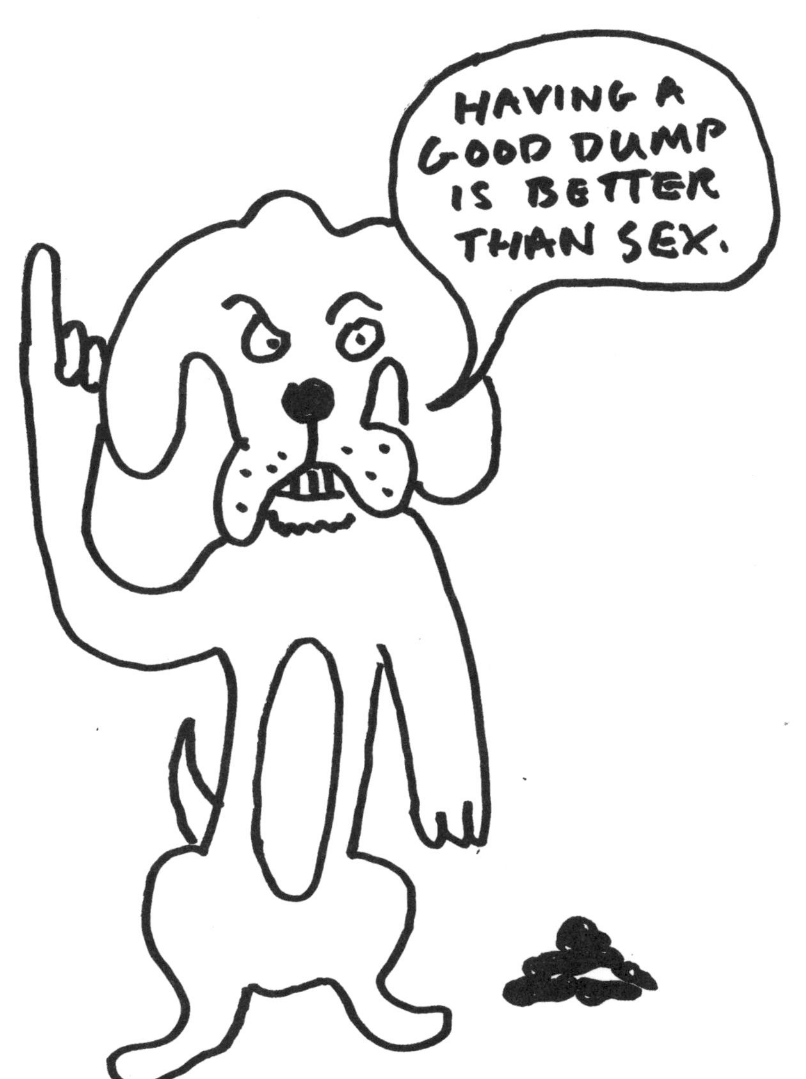

ACHE'S? PAIN'S? HEARTBURN?
THEN TAKE SOLACE IN

FRIDA KAHLO

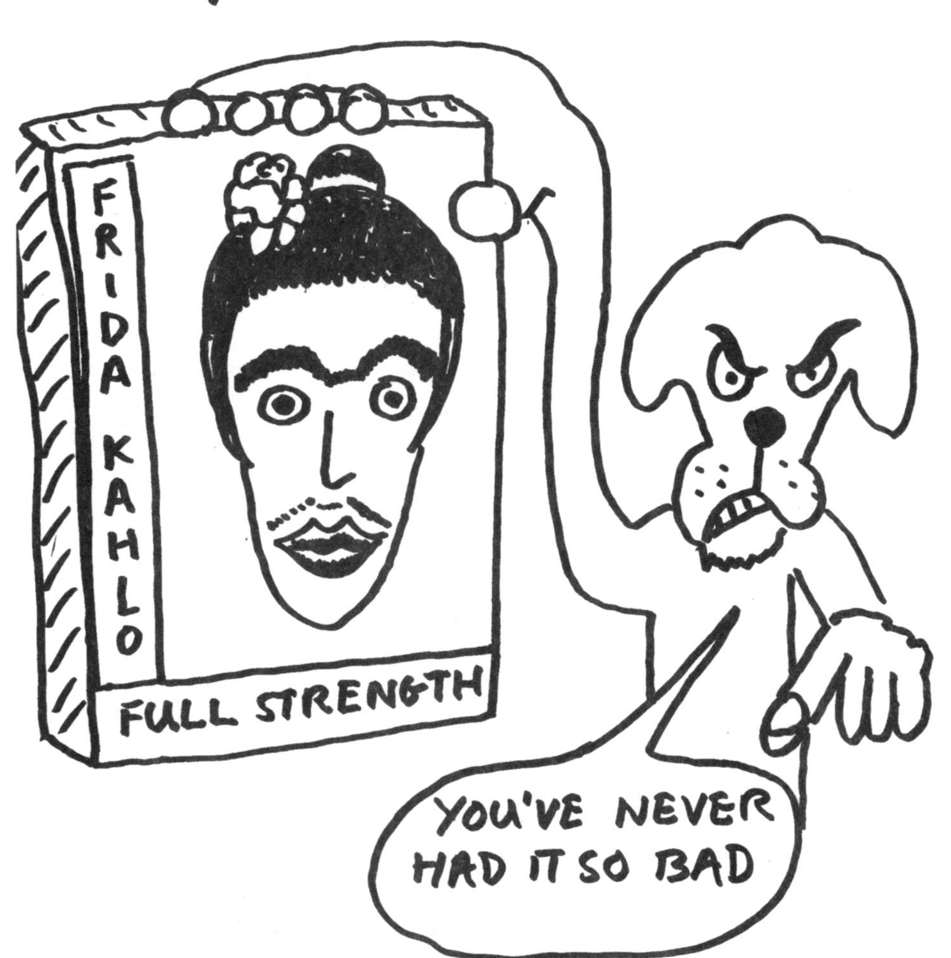

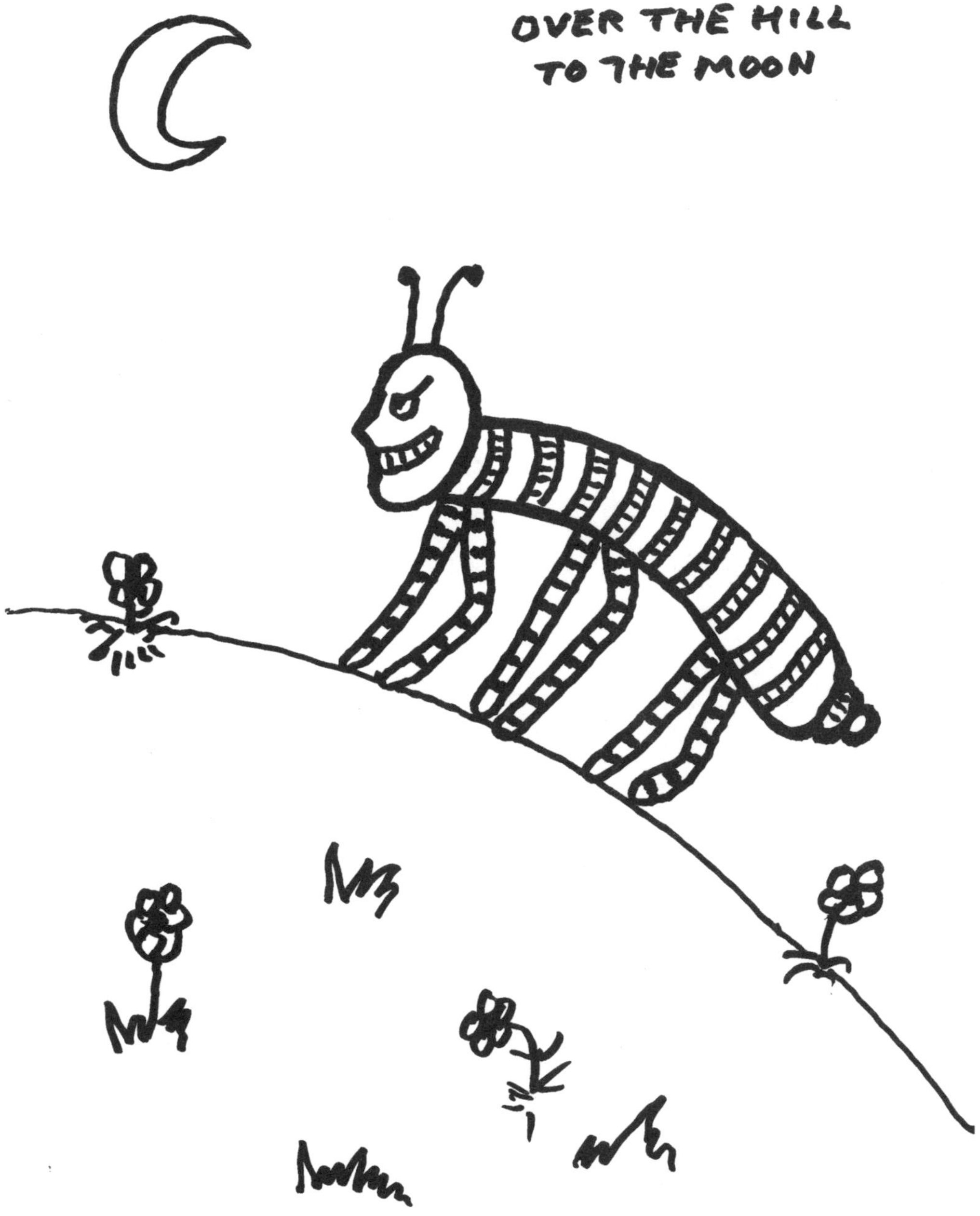

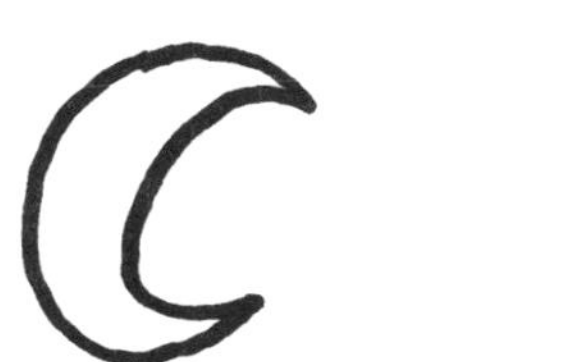

OVER THE HILL
TO THE MOON

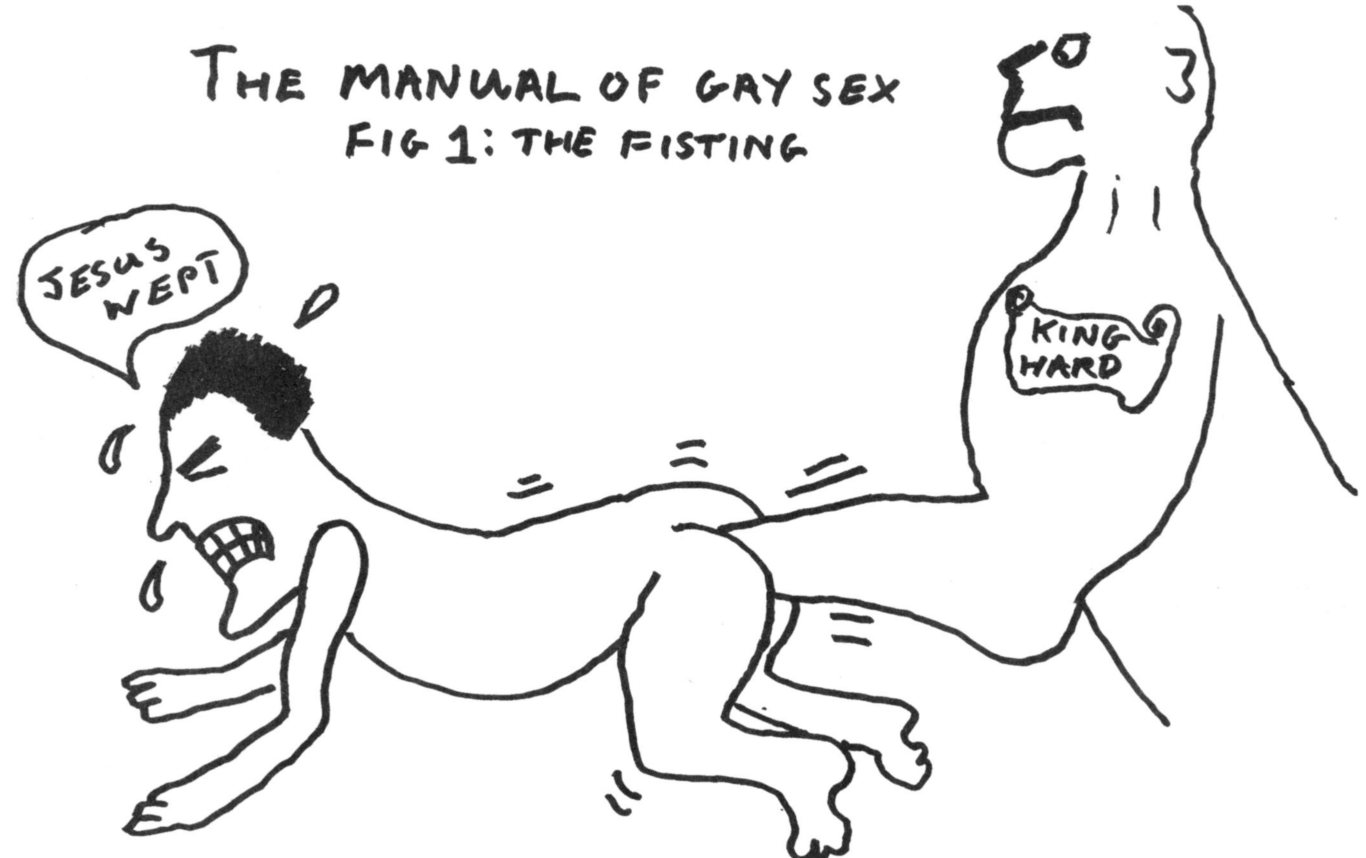
THE MANUWAL OF GAY SEX
FIG 1: THE FISTING
JESUS WEPT
KING HARD

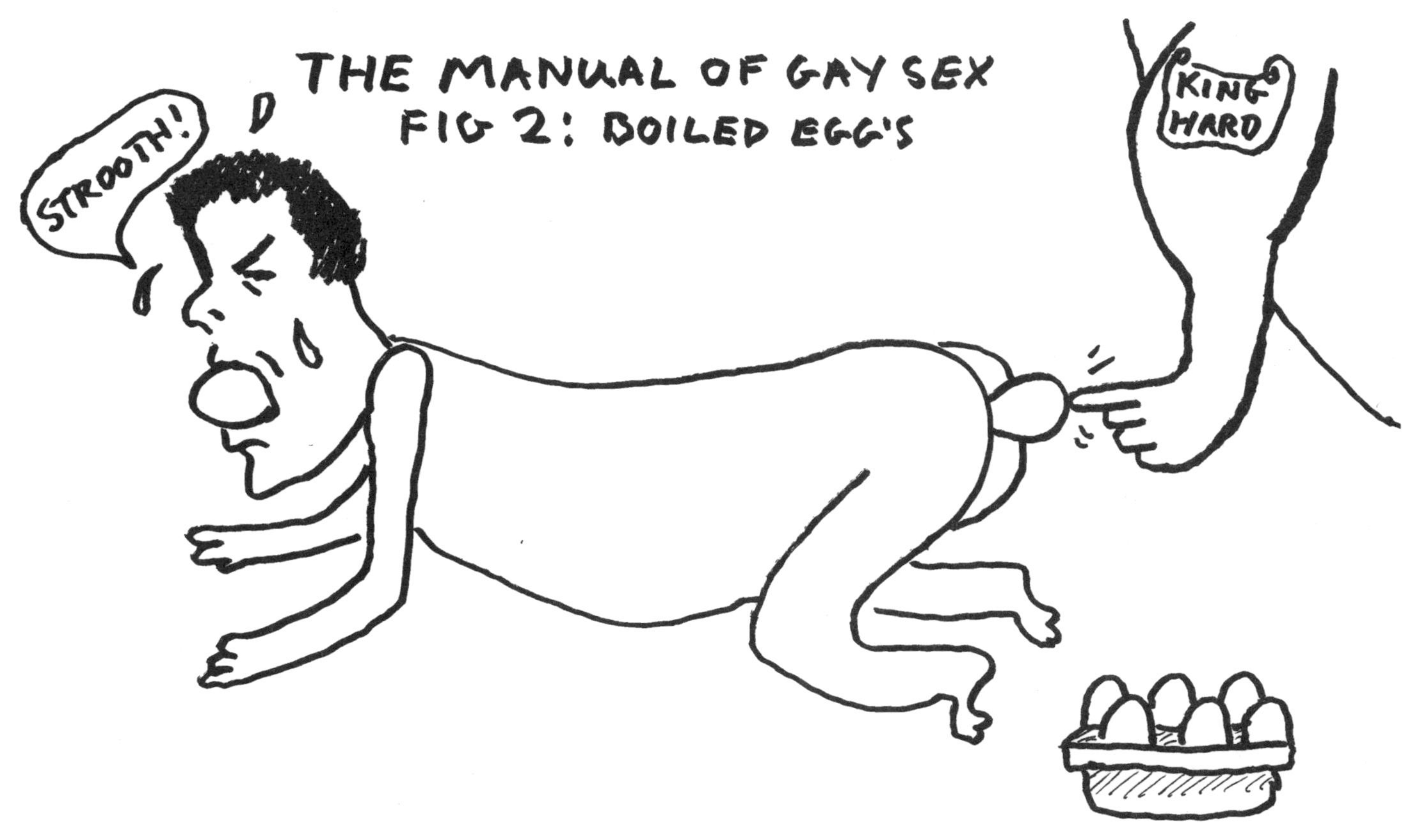
THE MANUAL OF GAY SEX
FIG 2: BOILED EGG'S
STROOTH!
KING HARD

THE MANUAL OF GAY SEX

FIG 3: THE WOODEN COAT HANGER

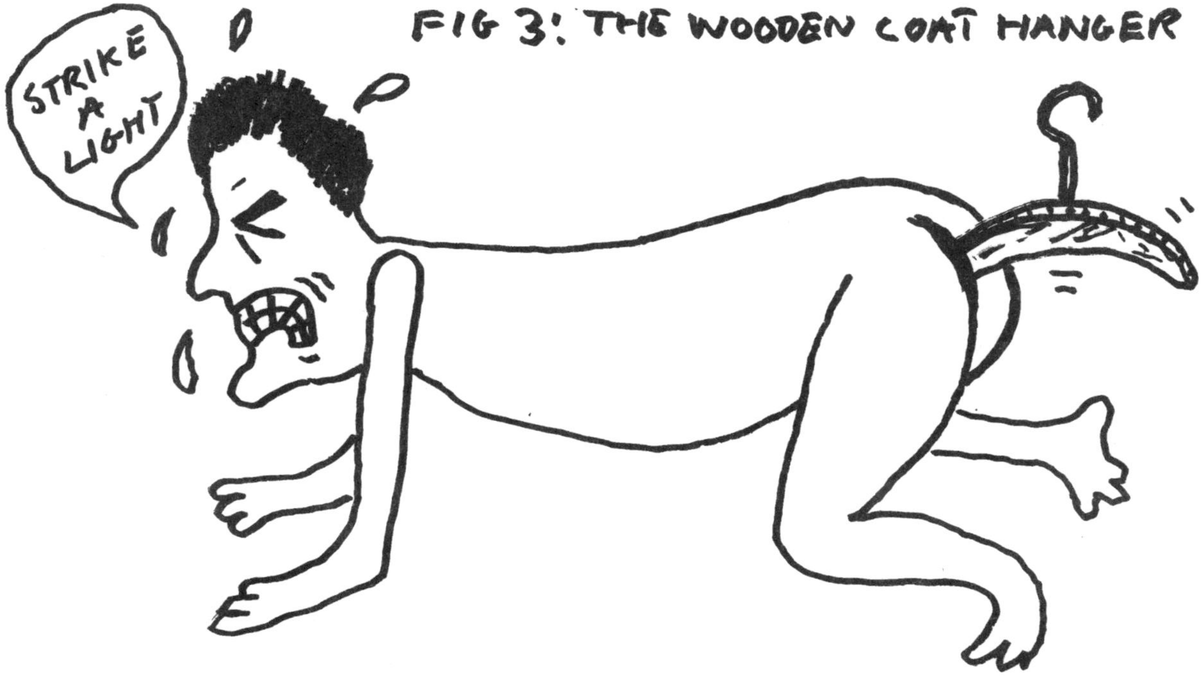

STRIKE A LIGHT

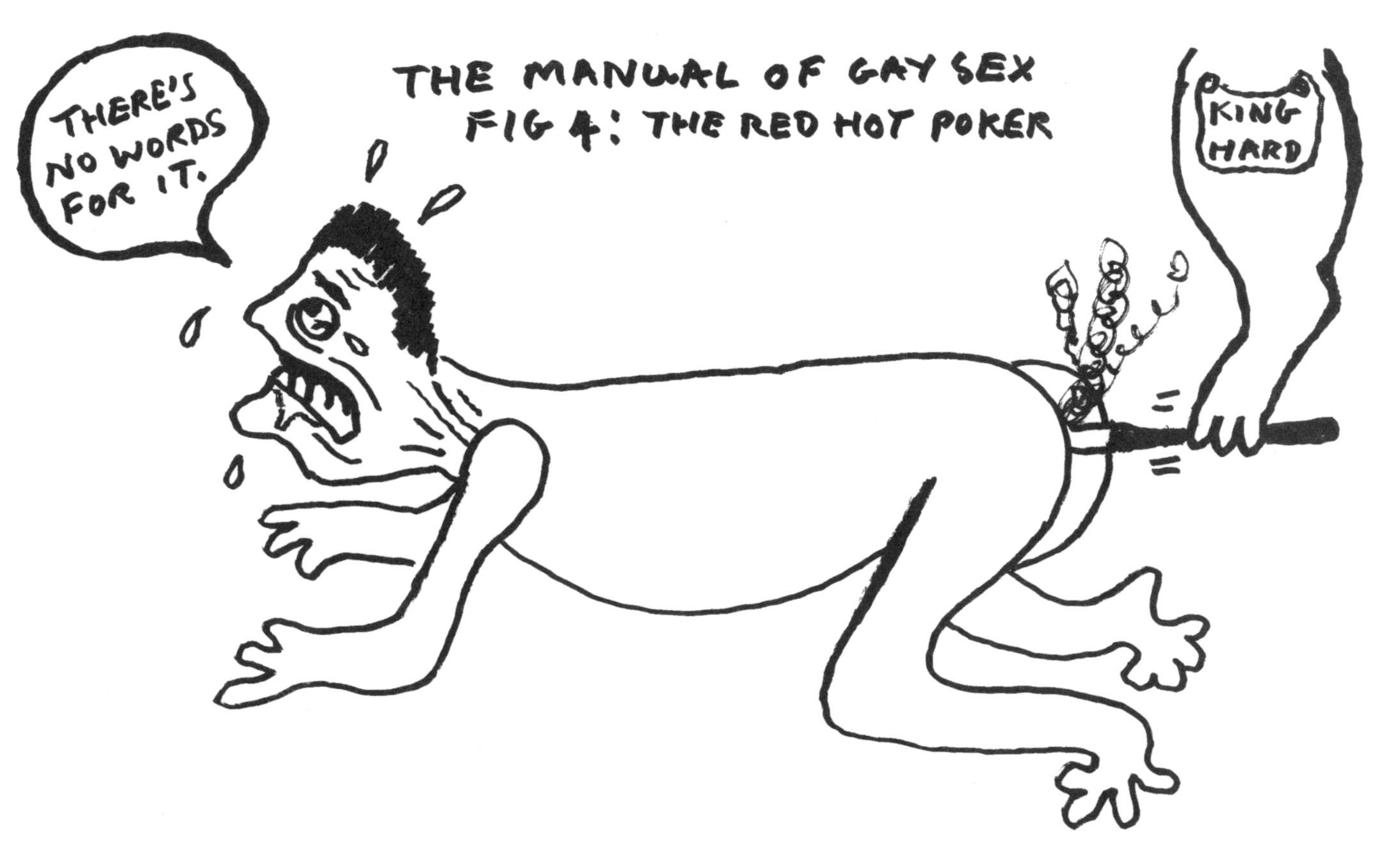
THE MANUAL OF GAY SEX
FIG 4: THE RED HOT POKER
THERE'S NO WORDS FOR IT.
KING HARD

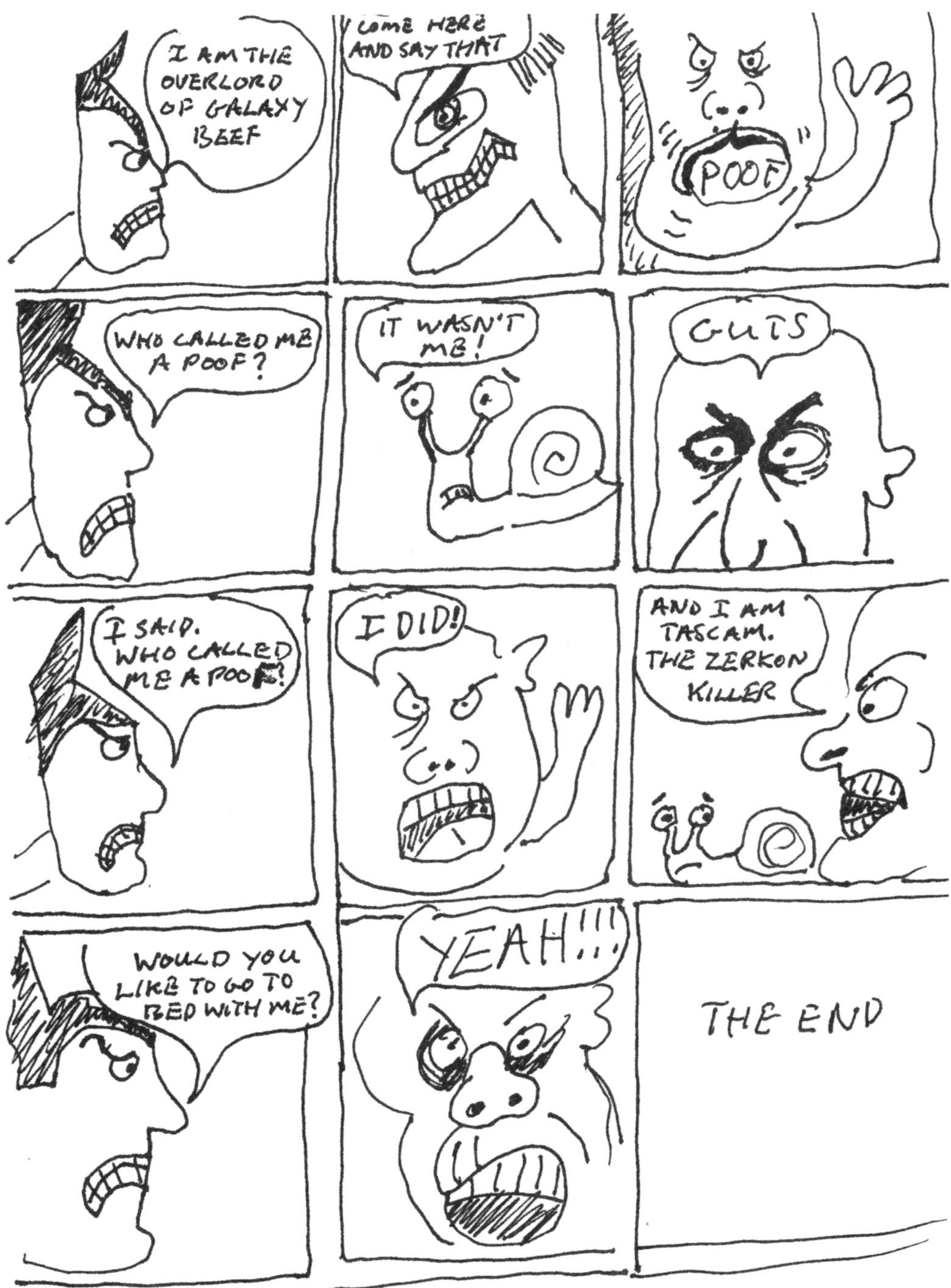
I AM THE OVERLORD OF GALAXY BEEF
COME HERE AND SAY THAT
POOF
WHO CALLED ME A POOF?
IT WASN'T ME!
GUTS
I SAID. WHO CALLED ME A POOF?
I DID!
AND I AM TASCAM. THE ZERKON KILLER
WOULD YOU LIKE TO GO TO BED WITH ME?
YEAH!!!
THE END

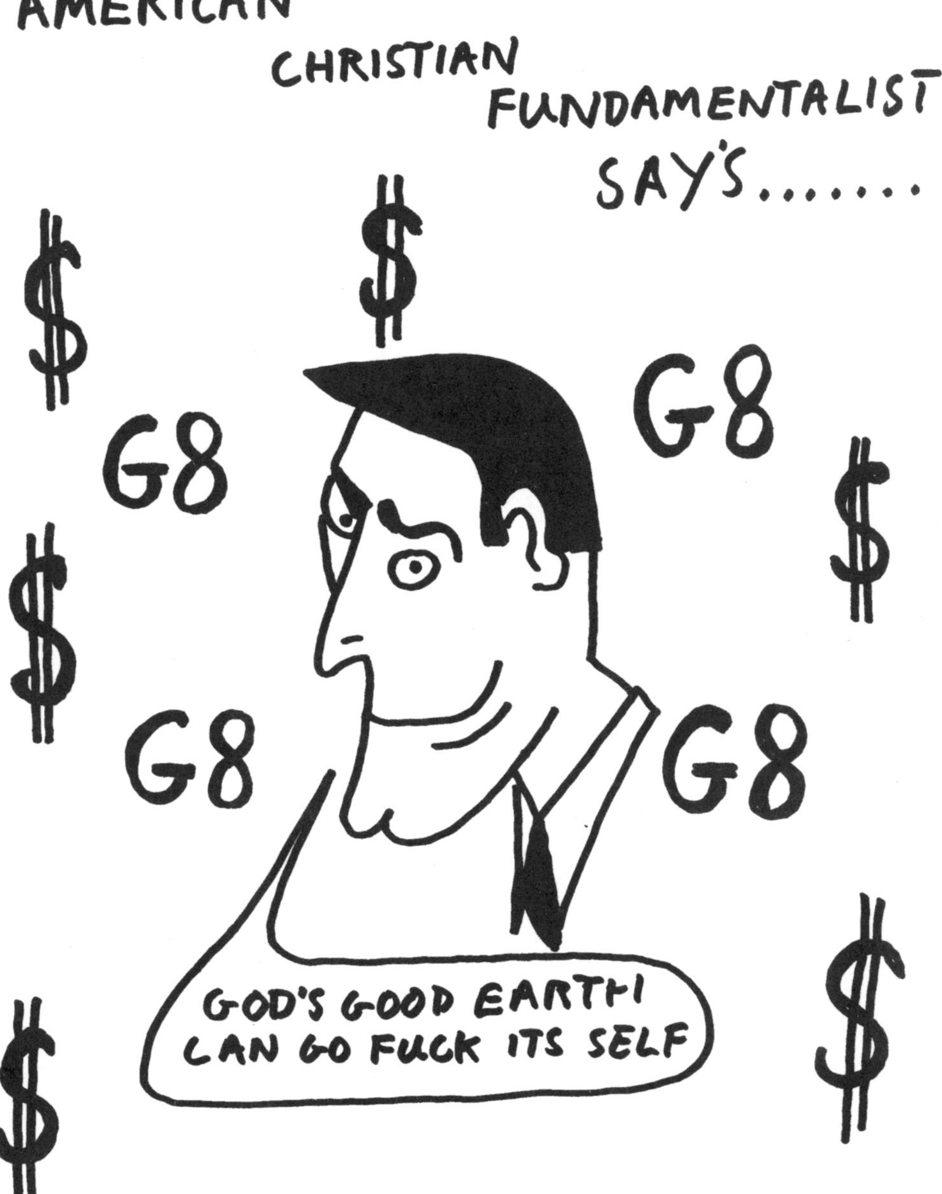
AMERICAN
CHRISTIAN
FUNDAMENTALIST
SAY'S.......
G8
G8
G8
G8
GOD'S GOOD EARTH
CAN GO FUCK ITS SELF

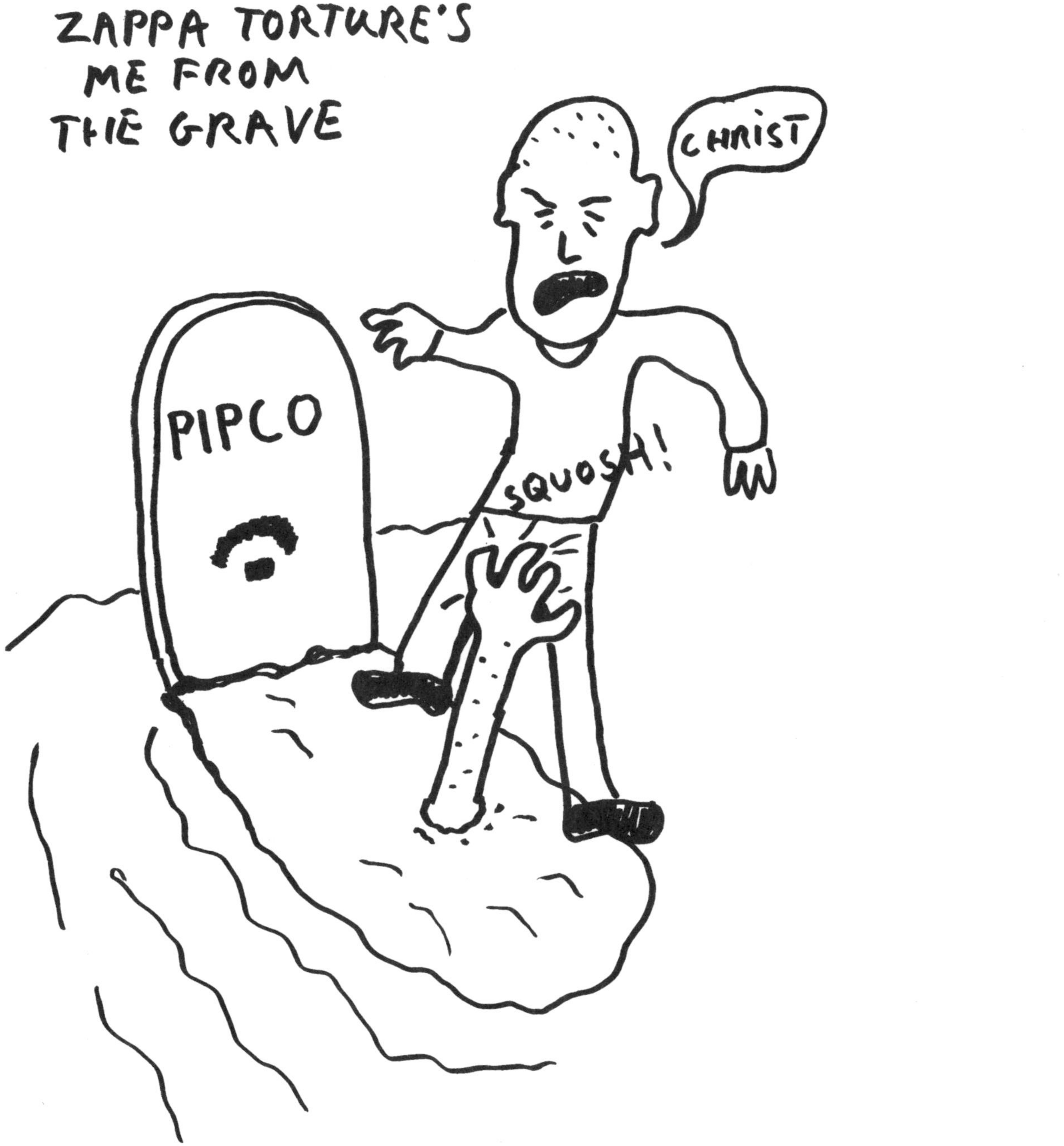

ZAPPA TORTURE'S
ME FROM
THE GRAVE

CHRIST

PIPCO

SQUOSH!

KURT COBAIN HURTS HIMSELF

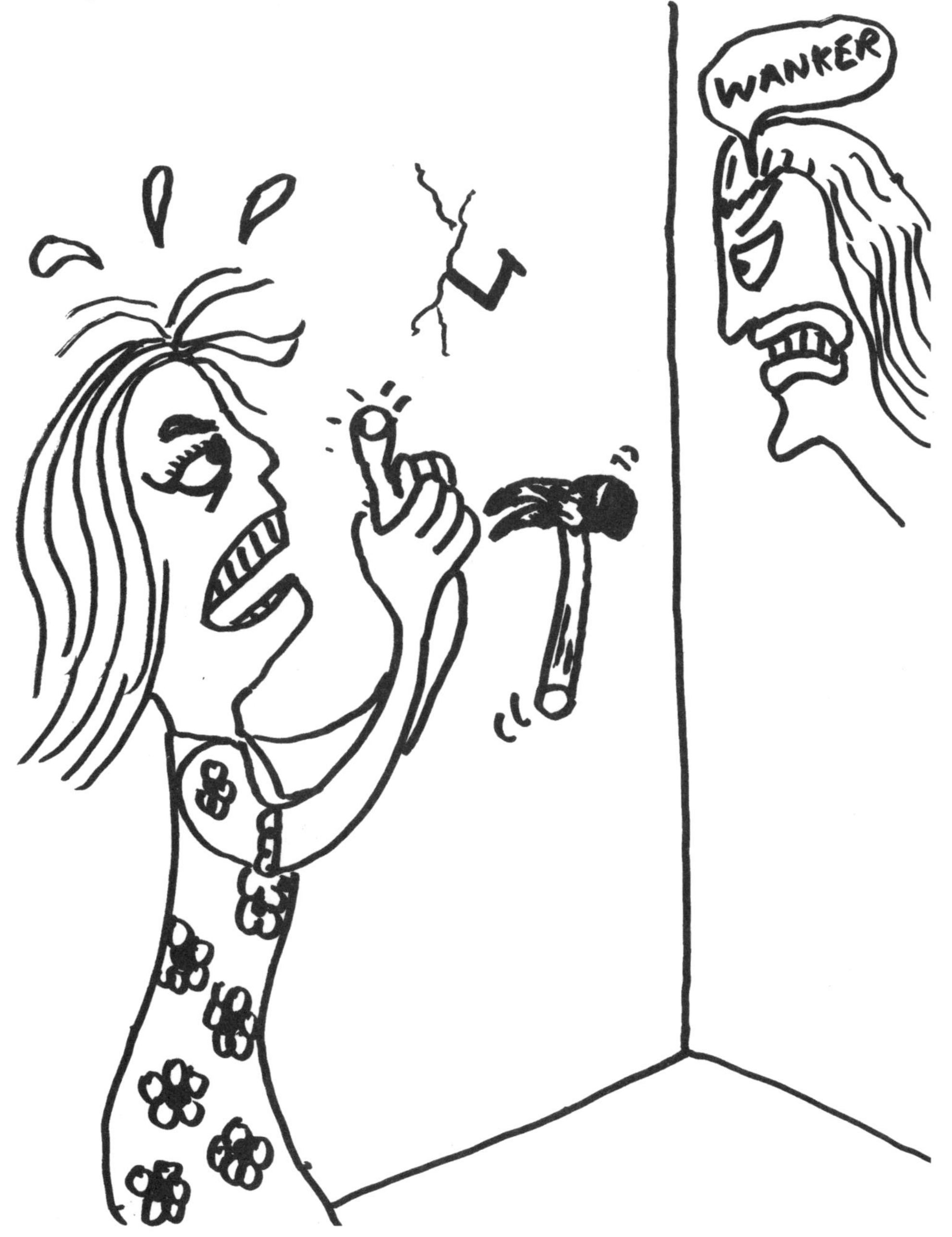

WISE MUTT SAYS...

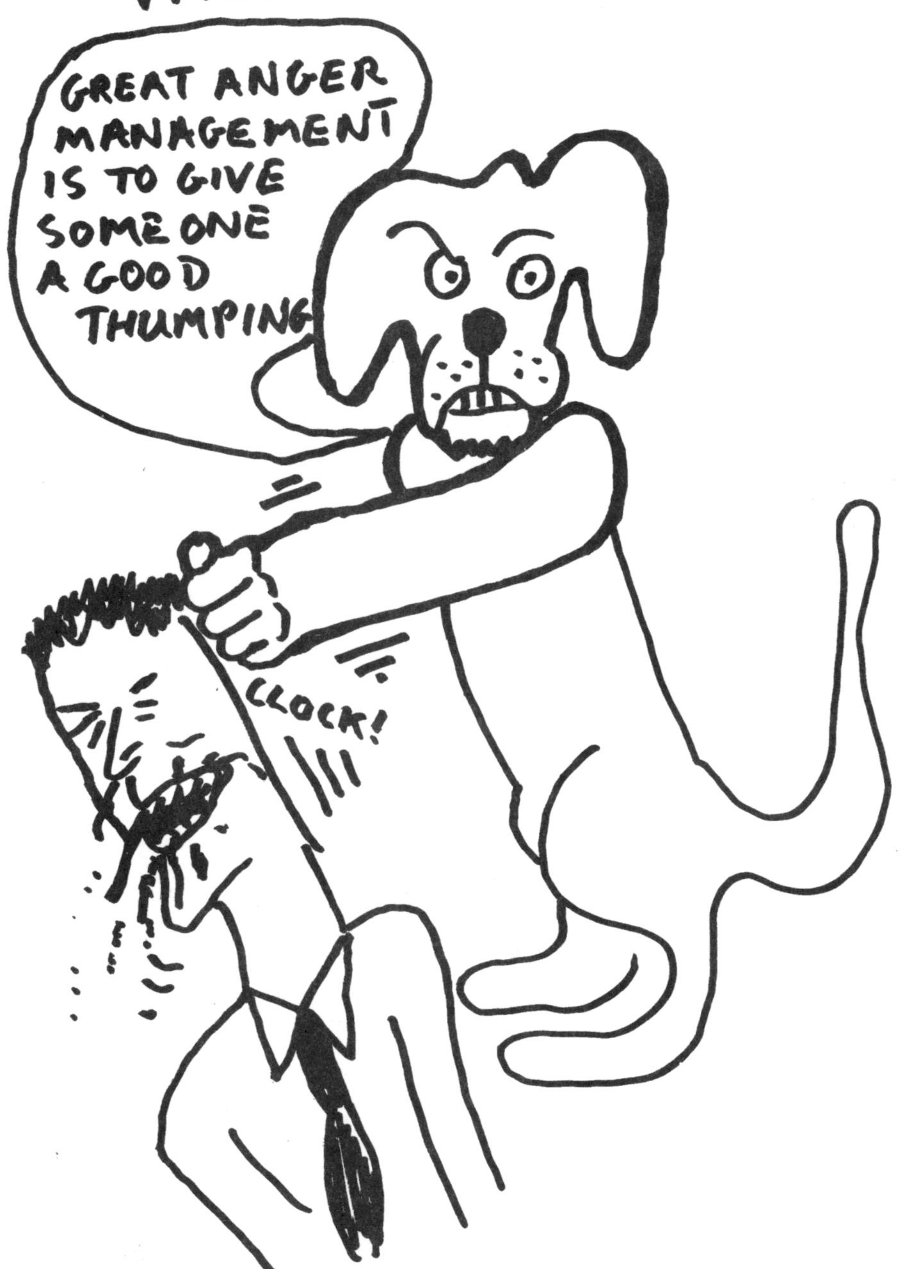

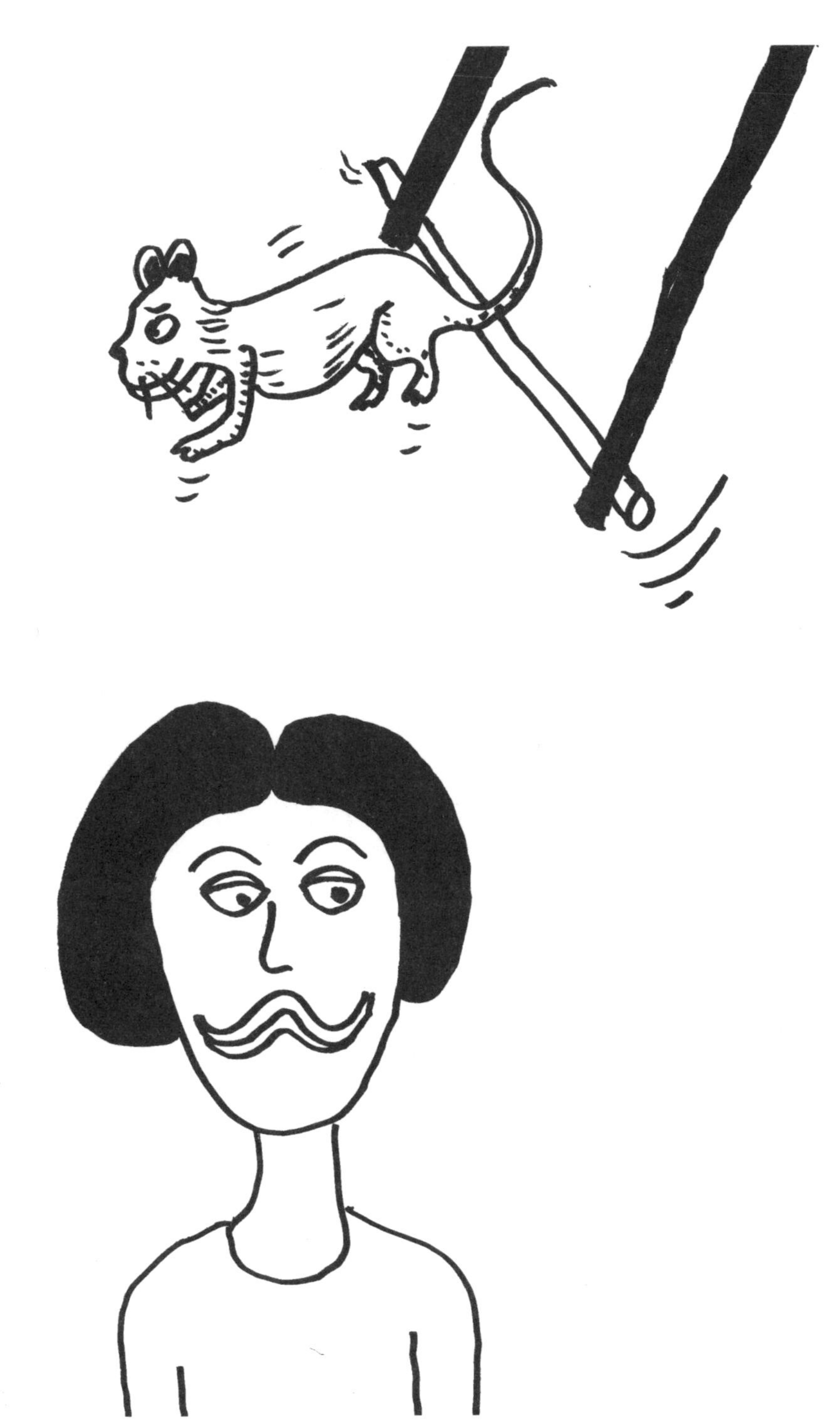

RODREGO: THE BLUES GIANT

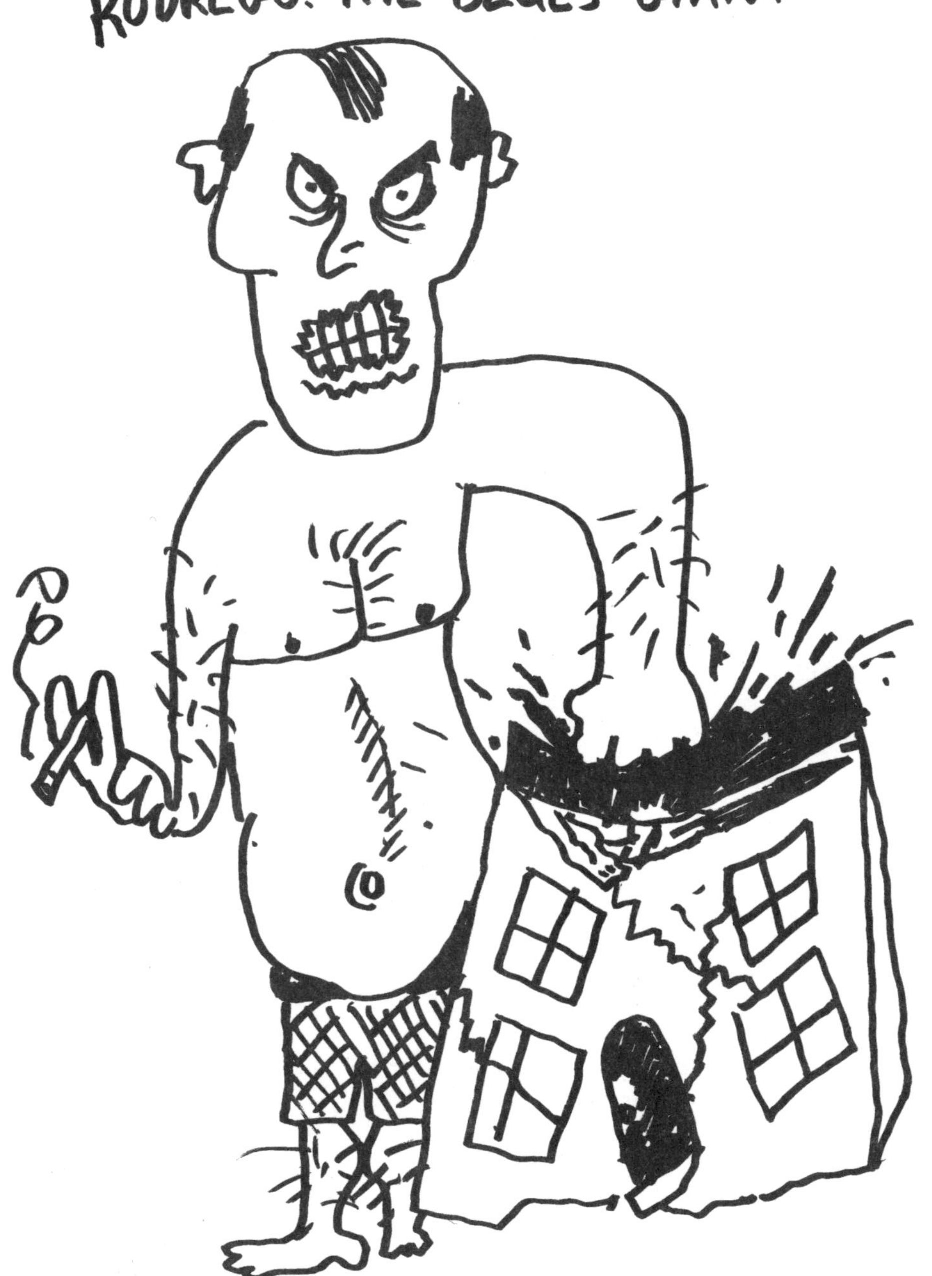

NUTTER TALKING TO HIS TV SET

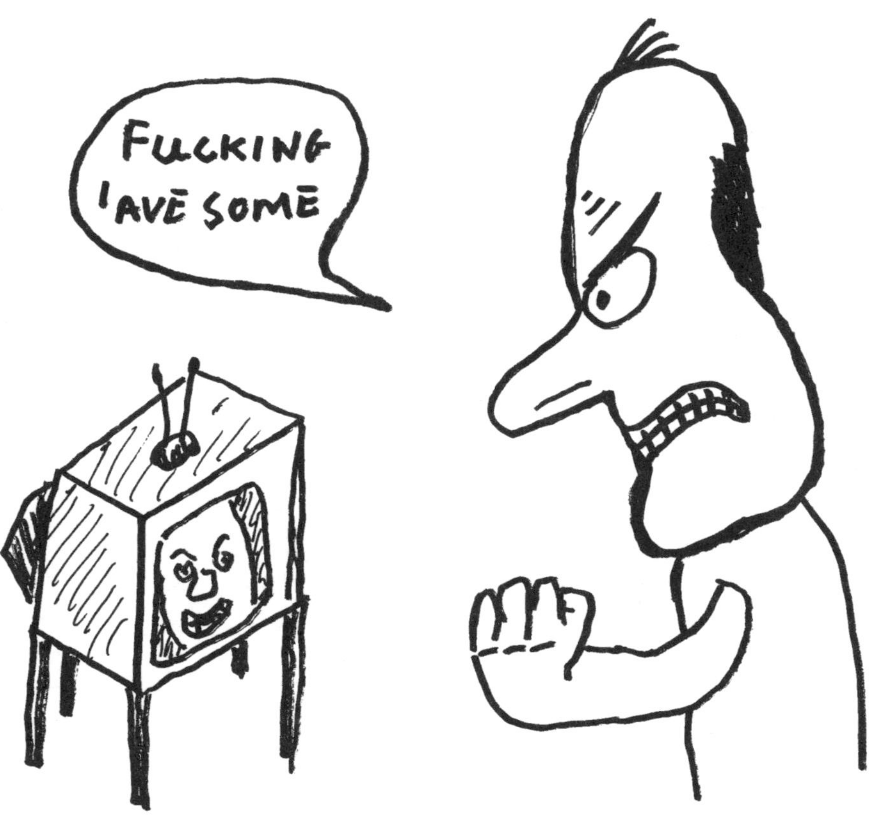

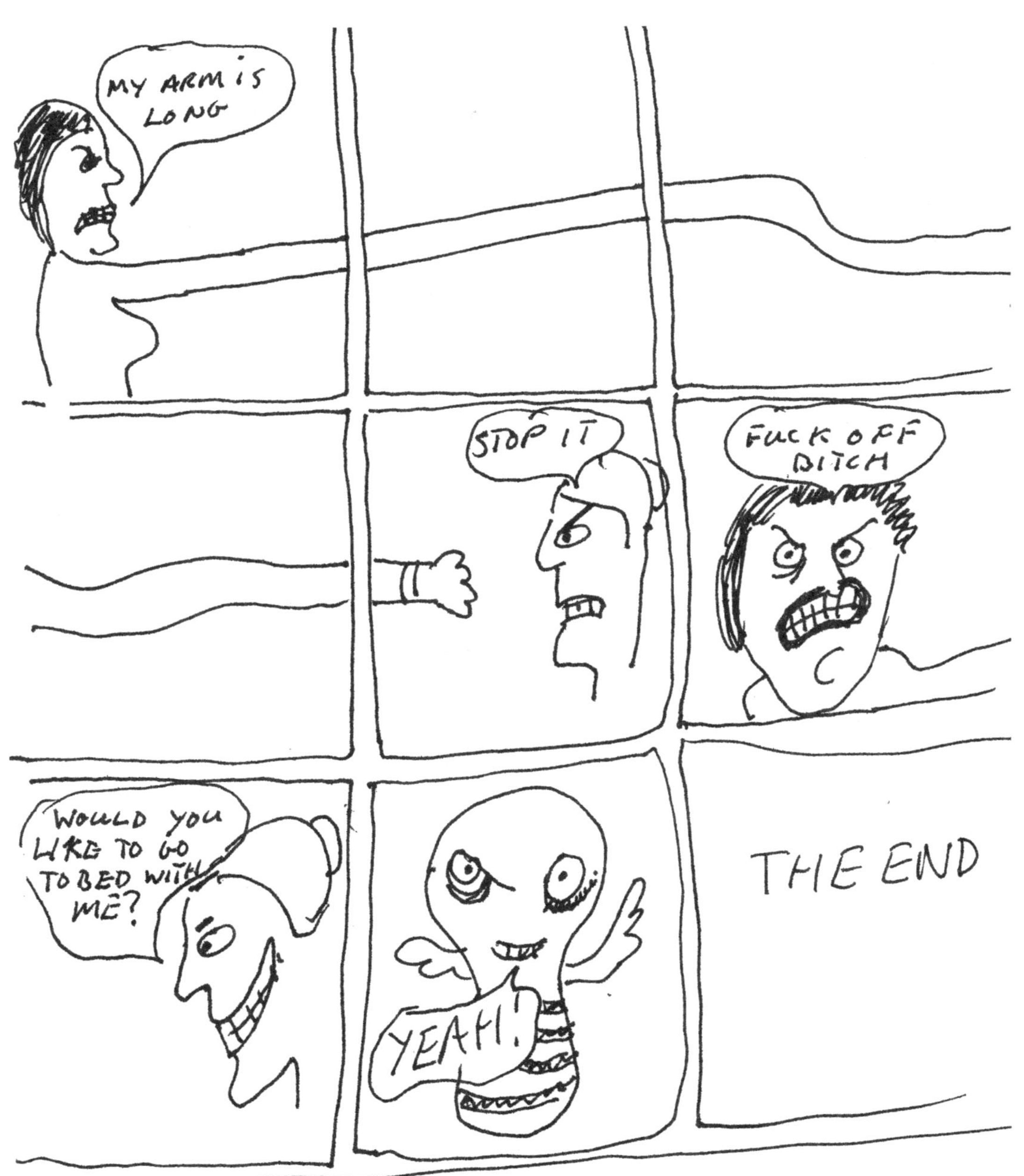
MY ARM IS LONG
STOP IT
FUCK OFF BITCH
WOULD YOU LIKE TO GO TO BED WITH ME?
YEAH!
THE END

HAIR STYLES No 1

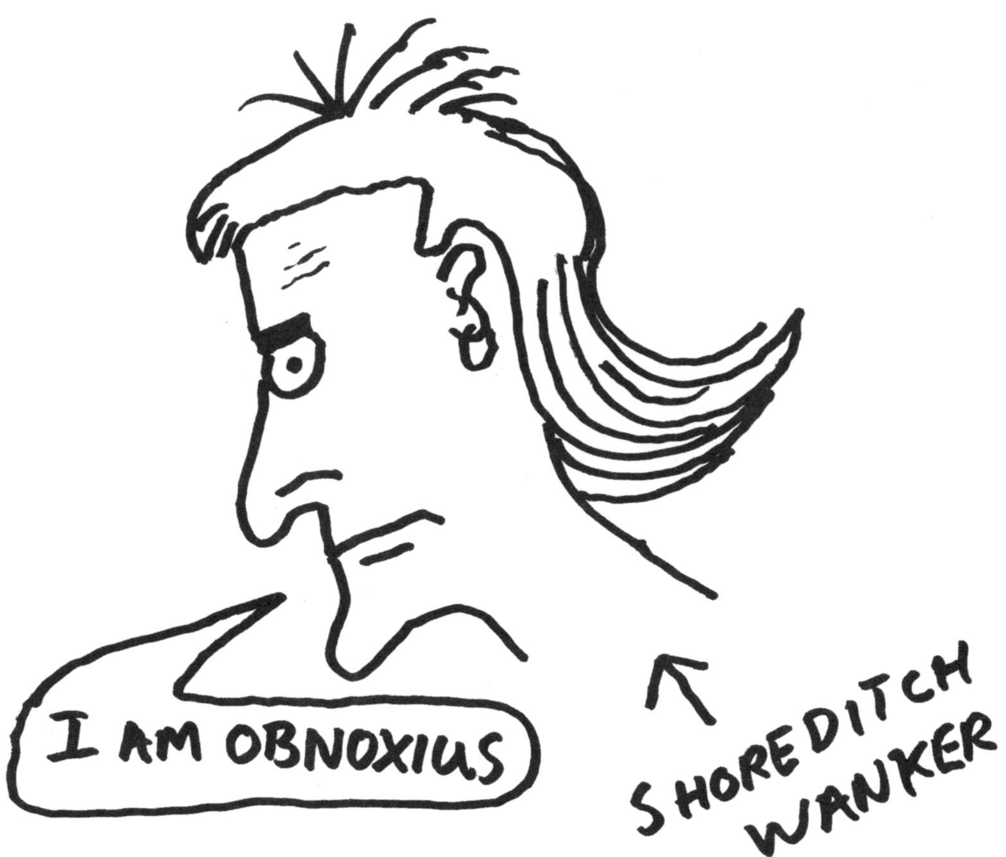

HAIR STYLE'S No 2

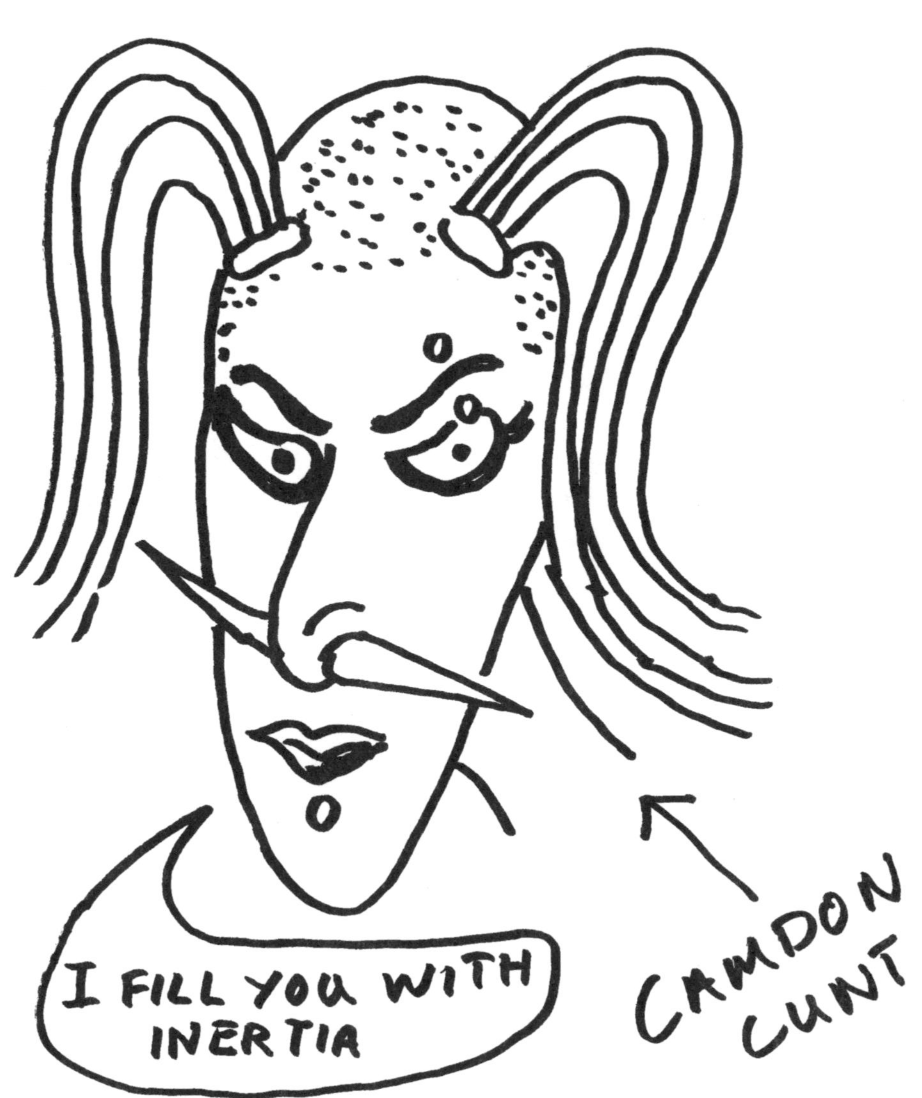

HAIR STYLES No 3

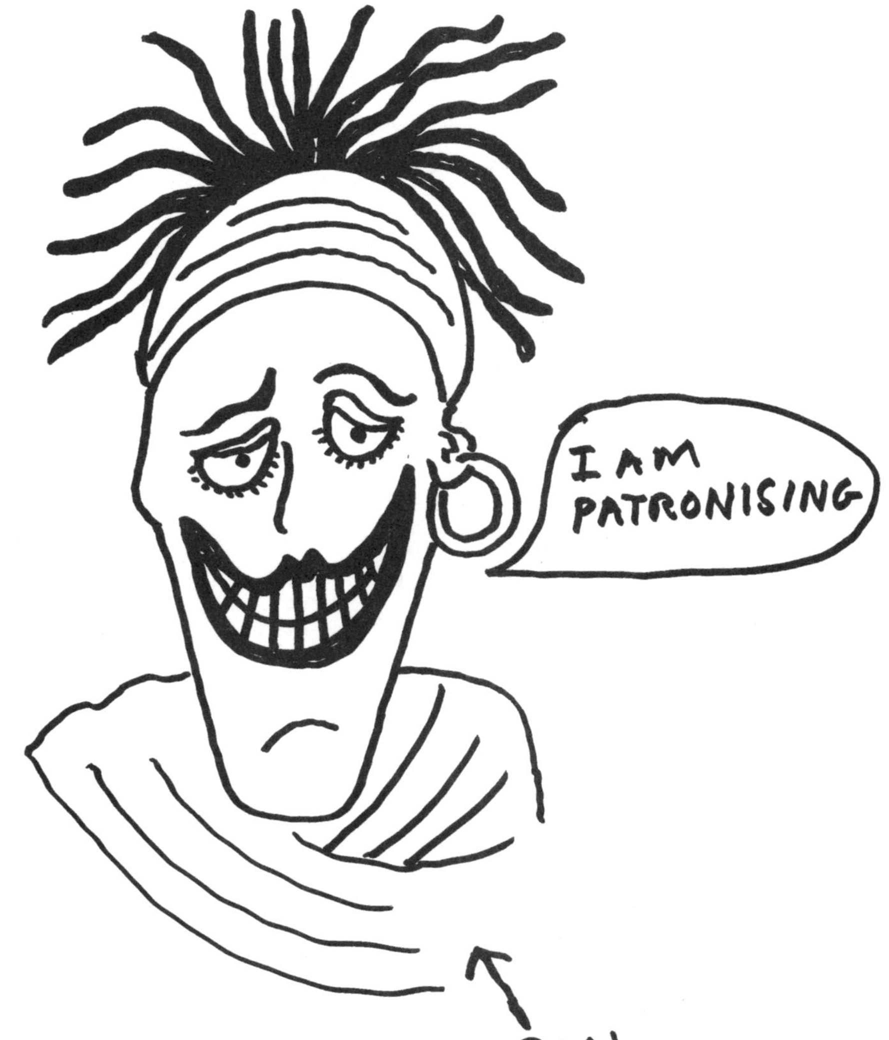

STOKE NEWINGTON
NEW AGE TWAT

MISTRESS OF KNOB'S

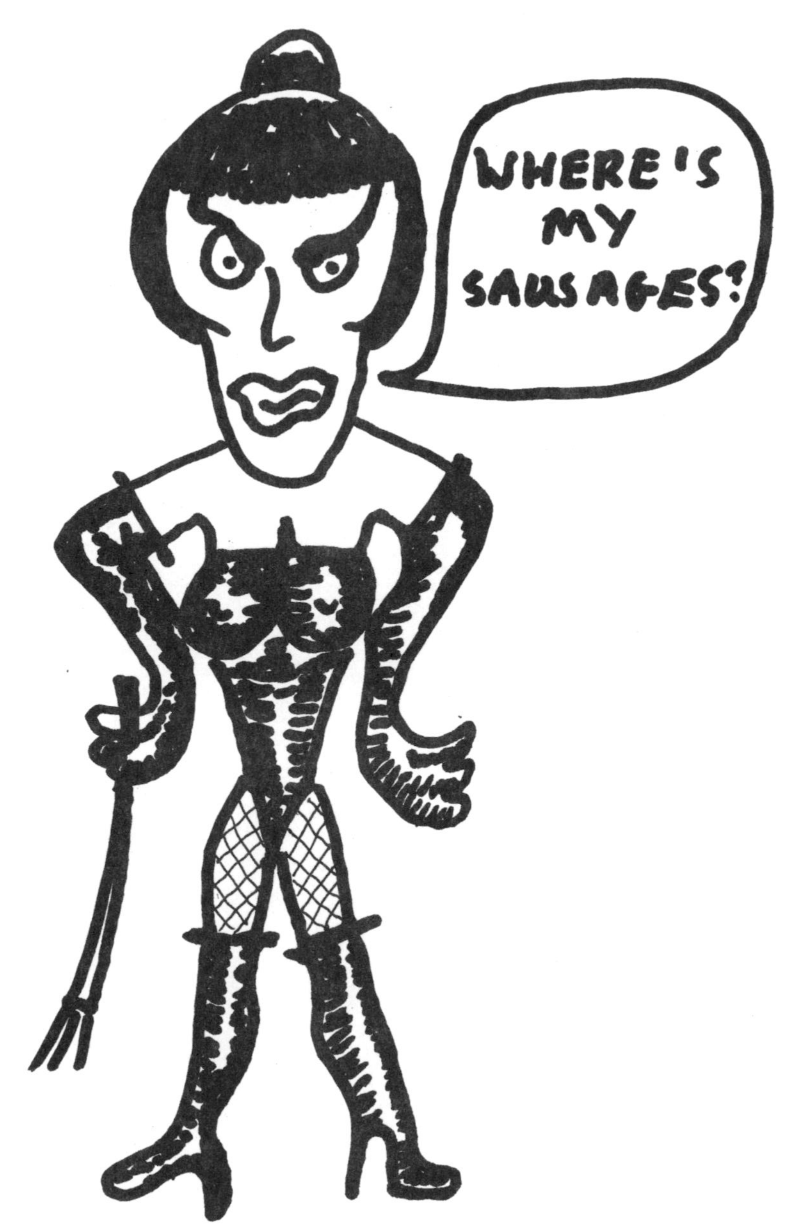

ABDOMIN FIGHTING

SWETTY BELLY BUTTON
VS
TROJAN GUT

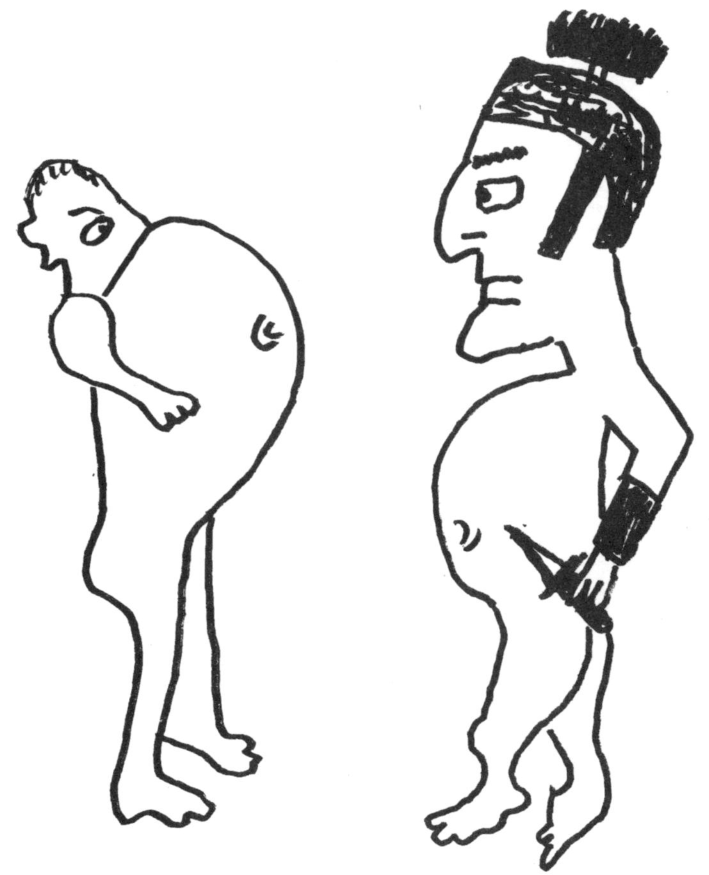

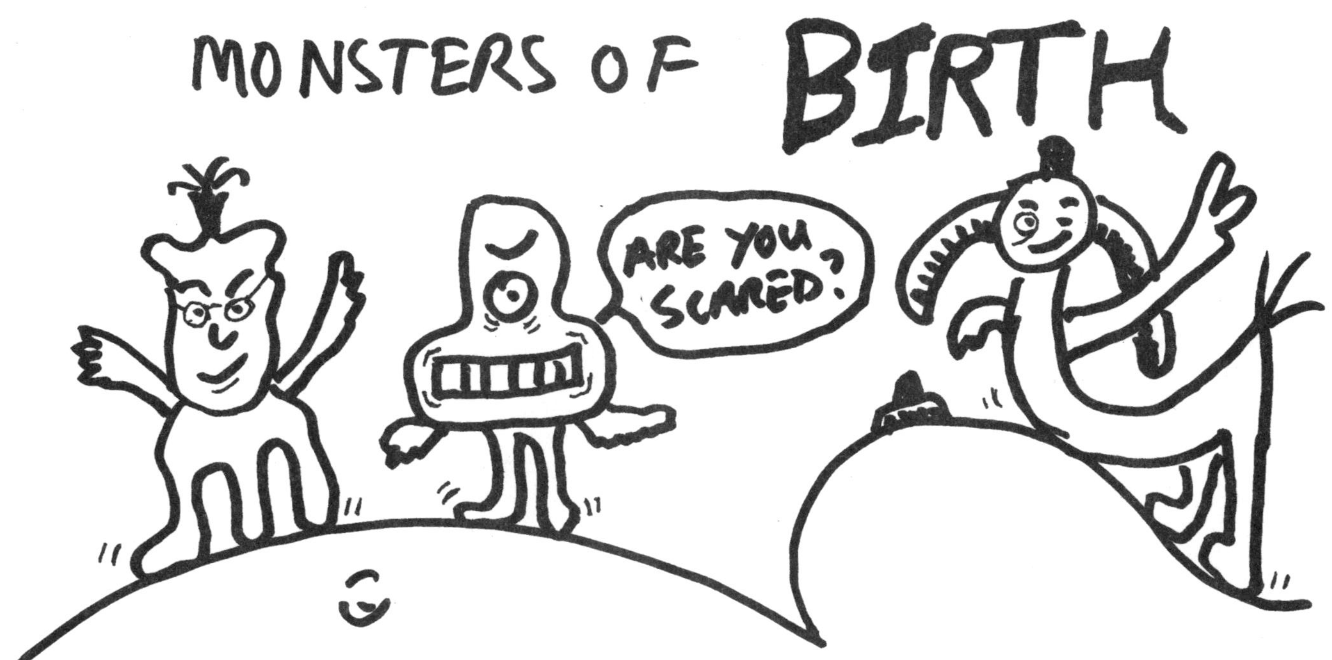
MONSTERS OF BIRTH
ARE YOU SCARED?

Sexton Ming now runs Rim Records, shows his work regularly at the aquarium's London and Berlin galleries, and looks after his daughter Lucy.

If you'd like to buy prints of the drawings in this book please visit www.theaquariumonline.co.uk